GROW YOUR GIFT SHOP BUSINESS: LEARN PINTEREST STRATEGY

KERRIE LEGEND

GROW YOUR GIFT SHOP BUSINESS: LEARN PINTEREST STRATEGY
Copyright © 2017 by Kerrie Legend.

All rights reserved. Printed in the United States of America. No part of this book may be used or reproduced in any manner whatsoever without written permission except in the case of brief quotations em- bodied in critical articles or reviews.

For information contact :

2900 Government Way

Cœur d'Alene, ID

http://www.kerrielegend.com

Book and Cover design by Kerrie Legend

ISBN: 978-1548559267

First Edition: June 2017

10 9 8 7 6 5 4 3 2 1

PREFACE

This is an exciting book for those of you that want free website traffic and to build your follower base. Because this book requires some reflection and "work" (gasp!), I've put together some handouts for you which were built for the course, as well. This book has been modified from my course, and if you'd like to take the full course to get the full aspect of all the software including screenprints and discussion, you're encouraged to do that.

The course is available for purchase on my website at kerrielegend.com. The Pinterest course covers everything in this book and more. Tailwind and BoardBooster and how to use both to achieve your goals for a solid strategy. I've been told numerous times by pinners that my book and the course is the most comprehensive instruction you will find on the web. That's good news for you, if you're just developing an interest on Pinterest. You're in the right place.

The handouts are available at:

kerrielegend.com/pinterest-handouts

The password for access to the files is the first word of the second paragraph of chapter 5 (all lowercase). I encourage you to download those as they are referenced within this book and are designed to help you.

This book is for anyone – it doesn't matter if you're a local business focused on services and want to grow or expand so you can stop trading dollars for hours, or an amazing infopreneur who wants to use Pinterest and learn the strategy to be seen even more. All are welcome!

Let's get started!

RESOURCES

WWW.KERRIELEGEND.COM

WWW.KERRIELEGEND.COM/PINTEREST-HANDOUTS

WWW.KERRIELEGEND.COM/TEMPLATES

   (get all my Pinterest templates here)

WWW.BOARDBOOSTER.COM/INVITE/SW3A9

(get free stuff!)

HTTPS://WWW.TAILWINDAPP.COM/BLOGGER-SMALL-BUSINESS

(get a free month of pinning!)

CONTENTS

CHAPTER ONE 1

CHAPTER TWO 11

CHAPTER THREE 17

CHAPTER FOUR 33

CHAPTER FIVE 38

CHAPTER SIX 45

CHAPTER SEVEN 52

CHAPTER EIGHT 61

CHAPTER NINE 72

CHAPTER TEN 78

CHAPTER ELEVEN 86

CHAPTER TWELVE 94

CHAPTER THIRTEEN 98

CHAPTER FOURTEEN 104

CHAPTER FIFTEEN 117

CHAPTER SIXTEEN 124

CHAPTER SEVENTEEN 128

ABOUT THE AUTHOR 134

ACKNOWLEDGMENTS 135

LEARN PINTEREST STRATEGY

CHAPTER ONE

Establish your blog's unique focus

Let's talk about creating your unique focus when it comes to your blog and the online segment of your business. You might be wondering why we're talking about focus when this book is all about using Pinterest strategies to grow your followers and make a ton of money, but before we even can discuss Pinterest strategies, your foundation needs to be firmed up. Your blog's focus is your all-important foundation. Without a foundation, you have nothing to stand on. So, let's nail down your foundation first to have a firm understanding on how we're going to build your business from there.

Why do we need to hone in on focus? Why do we care so much about focus with Pinterest?

First, if you write about a lot of different things and subjects, it's harder for your readers to grasp onto what exactly you're all about. One day you could be blogging about your favorite website to get ideas from and the next it might be about something that recently happened in the news. Perhaps you gained followers over your post about new ideas but they don't like reading about current events on your blog. You'll lose followers and interest in what you have to say if you're bouncing around on topics.

Think about this as you would an activity such as reading the newspaper. You probably have favorite sections that you read the most, right? Most people don't have time to read an entire newspaper front to back, and even if they do, they probably have their "favorites". They might enjoy the business section or even the arts section. Your blog operates in the same fashion. You want your blog to be that specific section of the newspaper they love and open every single day, and have them dying to read more of what you might share with them. If you think of the newspaper and your blog in that way, you can better understand the concept of developing a focus area, also known as a niche in some circles.

We can't assume that we can get away with writing about tons of different topics because newspapers are a whole different ballgame. We're individual bloggers, for the most part, and do not have the manpower to even take on such a task. But, as a single entrepreneur blogger, we can certainly focus in on one subject or concept and run with that.

Cater, in a way, to the person that loves a particular section of a newspaper. We want them coming back day after day to read. You already have them interested, so don't blow it! If you're writing about tons of different topics, then you make it hard for people to really grasp onto your site and love every single thing that you put out there. Sure, there will be posts that resonate with your audience more than others, and it's It also gives you the chance to connect with your readers consistently rather than having some readers who like your articles about cocktails and appetizers and those that like your posts about Instagram tips.

You really want to create readers who love **everything** that you do. You don't want to them to have to sift through your posts just to find something that they enjoy reading, so maybe they really like your tips on Instagram, but it's not worth it to them to have to come to your blog every day and hope there is a new cocktail image and drink to try out but then end up waiting for who knows how long for another one to show up on your blog or feed. Consistency is the name of the game with establishing your focus. You'll want to be consistent in your focus so that you give your readers what they crave to read and looking for every single time they visit your blog. No surprises unless it's a bonus download!

Here's the kicker. If they visit your blog from Pinterest, they probably liked what they clicked over to read, but they're probably not going to be interested in all those other topics you cover. I didn't just create this book to bring a ton of traffic to your site. I don't want to just create random visitors to your blog or your website, I want to help you create fans of your site and your writing; people who love what you're doing and are going to stick around for the long haul. The strategies, goals and tasks in this book will work by bringing lots of new traffic to your site, but it is so up to you to create a defined focus in order to keep them around and coming back for more.

Let's look at a scenario...

Many people, including major brands, have not developed a solid understanding of how Pinterest can really work. It's a search engine tool – not a social media platform. Therefore, you're pinning things that people might search for and want to try.

At first, people developed hodge podge boards with all sorts of things. Maybe they would sort them out with "things to try" or "goals for 2017". For the non-business user, it's perfectly fine to do it that way. But for a business or blogger, that's not the best way to approach Pinterest. So now, I'm teaching entrepreners a new way to handle Pinterest to make it work for your blog and business, regardless of what kind it is. So let's take a look at a scenario so I can show you exactly what I mean.

If you've ever been to one of my online classes, you might have heard this scenario before, but it's relevant and I'm going to share it here again because I think it defines and describes why it is so important to have a focus in an easy to understand way.

Imagine two blogs in front of you in separate browsers. The blow in the first browser (we'll call it Blog 1) is a cute, well-designed millennial pink blog that talks about all sorts of things: fashion, shoes, pets, interior design, gift ideas, cocktails, relationships, self-development, etc. There are a ton of subject areas and that's typically what you'd find in a lifestyle blog. Blog 2 is a blog about home womancaves and mancaves – designing them, building them, and styling for them.

Let's say you see a pin on Pinterest that has the title "Interior Design Tips for Womancaves". If this pin leads you to Blog 1, (remember this is the blog that has a ton of different topics), then you're going to love it. You're looking for ideas to make your own home getaway area – something you crave so you can lock the door and escape the kiddos for an hour!

Let's say you're really interested in learning more about design ideas for womancaves. You find the post useful. You'll probably start browsing around for more information on the same thing just to get second opinions or even more style ideas, right? But, wait. There's information on the latest gift Blogger 1 found for her best friend forever, a cocktail recipe, her latest breakup advice and finding the right man, etc. Then you start seeing posts and pins for her cosmetic business with links to an online store than has nothing to do with interior design. OH, and then there are posts and pins about her skinny wrap business and immediately, you're like, blah! It's not relevant to what you're interested in!

Now if the same pin leads to Blog 2, remember it is the exact same article, then you'll love the post – same as before. It's so useful and you crave more information! You'll have the same reaction and start perusing the Blog 2. You realize you just hit a goldmine of interior cave-building. Not only is there a free style guide and list of shopping items to collect for your new cave at home, but there is a collection of pictures and ideas that you can save to your pin board to show your spouse or partner for later. And even better, Blog 2 has a few things you can buy right off of the site and it'll ship first thin in the morning. How reliable! That's really how you build a foundation to sell products to your audience and grow as a blogger or business.

Because Blog 2 is building that foundation where they are setting themselves apart as an expert in interior design for mancaves and womancaves (aka she-caves), you'll come back to the site for more... knowing that it's reliable for what your goal is. You'll probably go back to it a few more times, maybe even make a purchase or two, sign up for the newsletter or mailing list, or visit often to get new, inspired ideas.

Now when you narrow your focus, you create content that your ideal audience can consume, rather than have to sift through tons of articles that are irrelevant to them. Remember – our goals as bloggers and businesses is to provide for an audience – our blogs and businesses are not about our own preferences or ourselves. They're going to go through a ton of other articles on your site and find a lot of similar and useful information that is relevant to them. You are going to become the go-to hub for a certain topic or niche.

This is super-simple and easy.

I think a lot of people really want to become the go-to hub or a more popular, more prestigious blogger. They want to have influence and make big sales. There's nothing wrong with that - and it is not that hard if you have a strong focus on your blog. People will start to turn to you and assume that you are a leader and an expert in that particular niche.

The problem is that so many people try to cover tons of different topics and it makes it really hard for them to stand out. So, you're going to need to set yourself apart as a leader and expert in a certain subject. You're also going to build an audience that trusts you, visits your work often and would likely buy from you. Wonderful, right? That's exactly what you want! It's the perfect outcome. It can only really happen if you narrow your focus, though.

For myself, for example, I've set myself apart from the pack by focusing on developing strategies through writing and design. People visit kerrielegend.com to see my articles because they see my growth, the productivity, and want to know more about how they, too, can be productive and develop a strategy that works for them.

LEARN PINTEREST STRATEGY

How do you find your focus ?...

We talked about why focus is so important. Now how do you find it? A formula if you will: your passion and talent plus how you can help or serve people, equals your focus. It's not exactly scientific by any means, but it works. Your passion and talent, so whatever you are good at, what you love doing, plus how you can use that passion and talent to serve other people, is your focus.

Taking me as an example, my talent is in design and writing sales copy through developing a social media strategy. That's my talent and that's my passion. I love creating graphics and showing people how to grow as well. So how I help is by teaching others design tips and social media strategy. So that's my focus; I focus on helping business owners and bloggers grow through social media channels. Your focus is so important because it is what is going to set you apart from the rest of the pack. Having a strong focus and a clear audience will make your work more memorable, shareable and profitable. You are absolutely going to win at blogging if you learn Pinterest.

I used to blog about goats and goat milk. It was what I did on our farm so I figured I could develop a niche around that. But guess what?! As much as I love my goats and farm and all the benefits they bring from a health standpoint, goats and goat's milk was not my passion. My own blog used to be pretty much your standard DIY blog. When I was describing Blog 2 earlier, that was pretty much describing me. I had a niche, and a small audience, but I wasn't passionate enough about it. I wasn't excited about my focus area. My boards had kind of anything that had to do with goats but there was no strategy behind it. I decided to really hone in on my focus which is sharing design, social media and entrepreneurial advice, and since then, my blog has grown by leaps and bounds.

Your homework...

Figure out where your biggest passion and talent intersects with how you can help your audience. Find a way to solve a problem. Get specific about what you offer. Don't just try to think generally; try to think more specifically about what exactly you're going to talk about. Define specific categories, topics, and posts that you will write in order to attract that certain audience and serve them in a really relevant way. Schedule them out so you can start designing your pins straight away.

You could also brainstorm products or services that you can offer, as well. Remember to get specific with your ideas.

Now would be a good time to decide: What do I want to be the go-to hub for? If somebody was writing a blog post titled "My Favorite (fill in the blank) Blogs", maybe you write a baby blog, so "My Favorite Baby Blogs". What do you want to be the go-to hub for? Maybe you are the go-to hub for toy buying advice or style for baby gear. You really want to get specific about what you want to be the go-to hub for, and then just imagine those types of blog posts where somebody is writing about their favorite types of blogs in a certain specific niche and what they would say about your blog. So answer the question: What do you want to be the go-to hub for?

Just to recap...

- A clear focus will help you stand out and create raving fans, not just one-time followers or visitors, but visitors that will come back for more because they crave what you have to say.
- We don't just want people to click over to your site from Pinterest, we really want them to stick around, so make your website a "play area" for people to discover.
- Your focus is your talent and passion plus how you can serve your audience, so be sure to define what your talents are and what your passion is. Sometimes we are great at doing certain things but that doesn't mean we are passionate about them.

Make sure you check out the handbook, too, because there are going to be some guided questions to help you figure out your focus, audience and it will help you move on from there.

CHAPTER TWO

Let's get started and define your tribe

In this chapter, we're talking about defining your tribe. A tribe is like your online family – they will repin your stuff, come see you from time to time if not daily, and be your fans. Focus plus audience equals love for your blog and business. Tribes help generate that love. Those two things are so important to creating a stellar standout brand; focus and audience. Your focus and your audience go hand-in-hand, and those two things help you define your tribe and find them.

Many people have trouble defining their audience because they don't have a clear focus, so start with your focus and then define your audience based on your focus. Your tribe is waiting for you out there somewhere – so this is not something you want to rush into. It's so much easier to do it that way than to try and think who your audience is when you have an unfocused blog or business. So, start with your focus and then your audience is going to become obvious. The more focused your content is, the easier it will be to define your exact audience. The tribe will follow.

Answer the who question...

Who are you blogging for? To create a consistent blog, you need to know who you are creating it for. It's hard to create a consistent blog if you have no idea of who your audience is. Carve out your typical person you would consider as part of your audience. Don't think of your audience as an actual audience, that kind of clumps everybody into this big massive unknown; think of them as one person. This is even better if you know someone who is representative of your ideal audience. Because then you can create everything for that person, and have a litmus test of relevance and relatability. Rather than trying to think if it is going to resonate with an entire audience, you just have one person that you are creating everything for.

In your handout, you also have an opportunity to fill out an audience profile and answer some questions that are really going to help you hone in on who your tribe is. It's also going to help you define who that one person you are creating your blog posts for, so really work on that handout, too, because that's going to help you define your tribe and your focus.

Defining your audience...

There are three ways to define your audience aside from doing the activities in the handout:

1. One is to ask your audience something: do a survey. If you have even a small audience right now, you can totally do a survey on your blog or your website just to see who your people are. Ask a few questions like where they live, which posts they tend to like the most, etc. Basically, inquire with any questions that are going to give you a good idea of why they come to your website. Why do they come to you? What do they think of your blog?

2. Look back through your old content to see what received the most comments. If it has received a lot of comments then it shows that people are engaging with it. What received the most views? If people are viewing it, then obviously they are interested in it. What received any other attention such as the post that was re-tweeted a lot? It's also worth a look to check your Pinterest analytics to see which content does the best on Pinterest. Then you can tell which content you should be creating more of for your audience. (Surprisingly, in addition to my blog posts, my font pins have performed the best! Wow – who knew?!)

3. And then lastly in the handout, creating an audience profile and answering those targeted questions to help you

define your audience for your blog or website.

Now, once you know who your audience is, you can create content that they will love. For me, I started making pins and recommending fonts to use for designing social media posts. My pins went wild! My fans love them!

You need to know who your audience and fans are they are so that you can serve them to the best of your ability. Remember, this is not about you, we're not creating a Pinterest or a blog for you, because you are not your audience. You are creating this for all those people, those awesome people who love what you create that will be your tribe. Remember, this isn't about you, this is about them.

The second aspect of the formula...

Here's another aspect of a non-scientific formula: your passion and talent plus how you can help or serve people – the last time it amounted to your focus. This time, it equals your content. Basically, it's the same thing, your focus and your content. Your passion, your talent and how you can help or serve people equals your content.

Now, figure out the best content for your people: what problem are you solving for them? For me, it has been helping bloggers who lead busy lives create a time-efficient, productive social media strategy. I pin new fonts to use in their designs to keep things fresh. It works for me. But what works for my audience will not work for yours. So you need to take some time with this question. What's the takeaway that is going to impact their life? Remember, we are making it all about your audience. How are you helping them?

Make it share-worthy; if they wouldn't want to share it then why are you writing it? Don't be afraid to do what others aren't; ignore the competition to an extent. Gary Vaynerchuk has always been an inspiration of mine – he always stresses about not worrying about what others are doing when you're creating. Focus on you and what you can bring to the table. Put your stamp on it.

You don't want to go completely off the grid, but you want to make sure that it is still relevant to your audience. Don't be afraid to do what they are not doing or offering their audience. Don't be afraid to expand on their ideas or to try different medium if nobody else in your niche is doing it. Create the best content for your people so that you are solving their problems and giving them a solid takeaway.

Just to recap...

- Define your tribe so that you can create content that is exuberantly relevant to them. Keep it fresh and natural, and don't overthink your audience or tribe.
- Figure out what problem you are solving for your audience – ask, listen and implement.
- Understand your audience by doing a survey, researching your old popular content and creating an

audience profile by using an ideal person in mind to humanize it a bit.

You can then create content that is very relevant to your followers, so much so that they are going to share and love and pin. In the next chapter, we're going to be talking all about how to create killer content. Now that we know our focus and our audience, we are ready to create some stellar content. So, make sure you also fill out those worksheets in the handout. Those are going to help you a lot in these next few chapters.

CHAPTER THREE

Developing killer content

As you may imagine, having killer content is a cornerstone of being able to rock it on Pinterest. So is having an amazing website (but that's for another book). In this chapter, we are going to be talking about what goes into creating killer content online and how you can use this strategy to your advantage to grow your brand and following on Pinterest.

Having a focus will get people interested when they arrive on your site, especially if that focus resonates with them, but you need awesome content if you want to keep them around. You can't just have a strong focus but then have bad content where it is not engaging or it's not interesting, or it's not really giving them anything valuable. Having a strong focus and then also having awesome content is important to growing your blog and website.

What goes into high quality content...

1. Create in-depth, lengthy posts. Think along the lines of the complete guide to X, where X is anything that is relevant to your brand rather than just posts that just skim the surface. Add screenshots, chapter, audio and/or research to support your post. Think outside the box. You don't have to just do text - you can add other things like graphics and video and audio and all sorts of media content that really helps your post to stand out. It also helps because people engage with content in different ways.

For me, personally, I enjoy reading posts, but other people I know love to watch videos and would rather watch a video than read a blog post. It really depends on your audience and the types of people that you are going after, so you want to make sure that you can mix it up so that you have different options for your audience.

2. Don't be afraid to do what others aren't. Sometimes I get questions from people who say there is nobody else in my niche who is doing this right now, should I do it or is it a bad idea? I

usually tell them it kind of depends on the idea but almost always, I tell them that they should just go for it. They should try to do this thing where they are thinking outside the box and doing what other people aren't, because that is what is going to help you stand out. Also, create evergreen content. Evergreen is a buzzword that basically means "timeless content", so it's not content where you are including a lot of dates or a lot of things that could be outdated in a month or something like that. It's content where somebody could read it a year from now and it will still be relevant. The content could be from the year 2013 and still be relevant if it's considered evergreen.

3. Add content upgrades to your post. We used to call these "upsells". Content upgrades are basically just additional pieces of content that somebody can get if they subscribe to get that piece of content from your post. You don't need to have a subscription model for content upgrades, but you could theoretically turn it into an email series. You could just give it away – but collect that email address – don't just have a download on your site without collecting information. For example, a content upgrade example would be like a free checklist. If your audience reads the post about some sort of step by step tutorial and then you could have this free PDF checklist that will help them in accomplishing the steps in your tutorial. You could give that away for free; that would be an

awesome content upgrade. It's a different form of media that upgrades your blog post, or what I like to do is to say subscribe to get my freebie or my free content upgrade. They are subscribing because they really want this free thing that you created and you are growing your email list at the same time.

Content upgrades are a way to create more high-quality content. When people arrive on your site from Pinterest, you want them to be wowed, because people on Pinterest are clicking over to tons of different sites every day. So why would they click over to your site and then stick around? It's because you have a strong focus and very high-quality content. You want to have that high-quality content to keep those people around and not just those kind of passerby Pinterest users who are just looking at your content and collecting one little morsel from you. You want them to subscribe, buy your products and become forever fans.

Now if you only focus on getting new visitors and don't work on creating great content, then it's like opening up a bakery where all you sell are stale muffins. Yucky. Basically, if you create a great focus, you'll have a focus, sure, but you only focus on getting new visitors. You're opening this bakery, and people are coming into your bakery - all these new visitors, but then when they arrive into your bakery, they're like, "These are stale muffins! Sure, there are a lot of them but it's all stale!" So they leave and don't come back. You want to open up your bakery online that people love, where all the muffins are fresh and steamy hot, where it's really high quality, where maybe you even have some new muffin recipes for people to sample, and some things that people aren't doing with their content. You're standing out, you're being unique and you're really keeping those visitors and turning them into fans.

Step 1 : high-quality content development...

It all starts with a title. Titles are important because they are often what get people to click through. Once you enable rich pins, they'll also be prominently displayed below each of your pins. The title of your post is going to be displayed in bold text below your pin. So you want your title to be enticing and persuasive and interesting in order to get people to want to click it.

If you are creating great graphics, your title will be on your blog post image too. It's imperative that you have a strong title so that people are wanting to click through. But do not overthink it. In fact, you should be able to come up with a whole month's worth of titles and headlines in five minutes. Great titles are persuasive, realistic. They don't over embellish, so you don't want to tell people a lie in the title, you want to be realistic. They share value and they're SEO friendly (Search Engine

Optimization friendly).

Basically, they include keywords or phrases that somebody would be searching for to find your post. Titles that tend to do well. So here are a few examples:

- List posts always do well; "10 Ways to Do Something", "Unique Ideas for Summer".
- "How to do", "how to" posts do well on Pinterest; "How I Created the Step by Step Guide to..."
- People love steps; step-by-step guides perform well and get shared dozens of times over.

Overall, lists and "how to" posts are very enticing especially on Pinterest.

Step 2 : high-quality images and design...

What kinds of images or photos will you use in your post? What brand story will you tell? If you take your own photos, aim to take them in bright, natural light. You can get great photos even with an iPhone if you're using natural light. Make sure that you have bright photos, crisp photos. You want your colors to stand out and you don't want to take them in a dark room because your photos are just not going to look as good.

Bright, natural light is really important, and then also telling your brand story, making sure that your imagery is consistent. Now if you use stock images, find images that compliment your brand. Don't use dark images if your brand is fun and upbeat. It's important to find stock images that also match your branding. Remember your photos convey your vibe, so make sure the imagery you choose is on brand. You want your photos to be on brand to really convey your vibe and that's also going to help you stand out on Pinterest and in the blogging world.

Some great sites for non-corporate looking stock images exist and they are some great resources for images that don't look so cheesy.

Here are a few of my favorites:

- Death to the Stock Photo. They have a free and a paid version.
- Bloguettes Stock that Rocks.
- Stocksy, they have a pay per photo plan. So do the other two, Death to the Stock and Bloguettes. They have a subscription model where you pay a monthly fee and you have access to all their photos. Stocksy is a little bit different, you pay per each photo but they have really nice, really high-quality photos.
- PicJumbo, they have free and paid photos.
- UnSplash, as far as I know, they only have free photos.
- KerrieLegend.com – I offer 1000 photos as your base and a quarterly subscription with unlimited access.

LEARN PINTEREST STRATEGY

You also get premium templates to design your photos for Instagram, Pinterest and your blog. Basically, my photo stock site is a goldmine and provides a ton of value you won't find elsewhere.

All of these sites are awesome options for finding beautiful stock images. Many of them are free that you can use on your blog posts.

Tip time! Batch your own photos. Batching works in all facets of running a blog or business, but the idea is simple: do several days of work of the same task all at once. Take all your photos for the week all at once in like an hour. Set aside 1-2 hours a week and take all your photos for the week or month, just get it all out of the way and batch it together so you're not spending 15 minutes here to 45 minutes there, you're doing it all at once, getting it all out the way so you can just set up your equipment, get it all done and have all those photos finished. This is going to save you so much time. It also works great for writing content. If you're having trouble getting your content finished, then just set aside a couple hours a week and work on your content so that you can schedule it out and have it finished.

I teach a different course apart from Pinterest on how to maximize your social media strategy and enhance your productivity so you can get back to being more creative and producing more writing. Or, more time for family, which is always great! Check out my website at kerrielegend.com to learn more about that course.

Step 3 : structure your content...

Honestly, you can be a mediocre writer and still make it as a blogger, (trust me I've seen plenty of them, even articles from great writers with mediocre blogs) primarily because many blogs don't only rely on writing. There are a lot of blogs out there like fashion, lifestyle, or food blogs where you don't necessarily need to be a great writer. Of course, it will help, but if that's not your strongpoint then you could still make it with beautiful photos and other components of your blog.

But, no matter what you do, your writing needs structure. People nowadays will look at huge paragraphs of writing of text and simply say "ugh". It's just. Too. Much. They can't process that amount of information. They're not going to read a huge paragraph of text. You need structure. Great structuring includes short paragraphs; try to keep them to five lines or less. You don't want to have this huge mass of text. Five lines or less is what you are aiming for, short paragraphs.

Use headings to divide each section, so that it's easier to scan your content and find exactly what the article is about and if they want to read it. Lists are a great way to divide up content too. Consider using headings in conjunction with lists. So, you can have point 1, 2, 3, etc. and create a great-looking, structured post.

Step 4 : create clear paths...

When someone arrives on your site, what do you want them to do? Make it obvious. Most people honestly don't do this and this is a huge thing for any type of website. You want to have a clear path. What do you want people to do when they arrive on your site? On my own site, I have a "Start Here" area. It helps foster sign-ups to my email list. What do you want them to do when they arrive from Pinterest on a specific post? What's the end goal? Is it just to have them read your post? Is it to have them subscribe to your Instagram account or your email list? Is it to have them purchase your e-book?

Think about what's the end goal of them arriving on your site and then make it obvious. You shouldn't set up your posts so that they read one and then spend five minutes figuring out where everything else is. You want it to be obvious what you want them to do.

Examples of some clear paths that you can implement on your blog:

- Add categories to your menu bar at the top. Categories with the most relevant topic to your blog that make it easy for people to view the other content in a specific category that they might be interested in.

- Include email opt-in forms in your header, below your posts and in your side bar. Add a bunch of email opt-in forms so that in case your reader doesn't see the first one, like in your header or below your posts. They might see another one like in your side bar or maybe you even have a pop up, so include multiple opt-in forms.
- Include related posts below your post to keep them browsing, clicking around, getting more engaged and interested in your website.
- Add social media icons below posts and encourage them to follow you.
- Include images of your products or services in your sidebar, letting them know how they can work with you.

These are just some examples of different clear paths that you can implement on your website to make it more obvious what you want somebody to do once they get on your site.

Speaking of clear paths, I want to share a clear path that I use on my own website. When someone visits my website, this is the very first thing that they see, and you can see the "Start Here" button on my menu. I get them introduced to my content and grab a sign-up. I also have a pop-up that says "I'd love to send you my resource library and give you updates!"

This is the path that I want people to take when they visit my website; sign up and get on my email list. I have different opt-in forms around my website. This one is the most prominent and the one everyone sees when they come to my site for the first time. I recommend brainstorming and really thinking about what that clear path is for you. For me, it's my email list, and just a little spoiler alert, it's what I recommend for you as well.

I think you should really focus on your email list, but maybe you have another path that you want to take. You just need to be intentional about what that clear path is that you want people to go on when they visit your website and then make your website geared towards having people do or take that one specific action.

This is not about cluttering your website with tons of options, side bar graphics, flashing banners and confusion. This is about zeroing in on what is that one intentional message and purpose of your website and how are you going to get people to take action in the direction of that message. Sometimes we forget all about that and assume our readers know what we do. Trust me, they don't know. Tell them. Make it clear.

Step 5 : what is the takeaway ?...

For every single post you write, you should be able to answer specifically what is somebody going to get out of reading this post? What's the takeaway? Posts with a strong takeaway or value are ones that get re-pinned and increase your followers and fans. People are not going to re-pin your posts, or click through to your posts if it is vague or hard to understand what the value of the post is. You need to make it extremely obvious what the value is, and define what's the takeaway.

What are they going to get out of reading your post? A takeaway can be that you taught them something. Maybe it's a tutorial, a "how to" post, etc. - any type of post where you are teaching them how to do something. It could also be that you inspired or encouraged them in some way. It doesn't have to be quite as tangible; maybe it's more of self development or an encouragement type of post. The takeaway can be a little bit less tangible in that sense, but you still want to be able to very specifically answer, what is someone going to get out of reading this post?

Step 6 : Give, give and give some more (plan on giving, for like, forever)...

So many bloggers nowadays operate under the idea that you can publish blog posts that are short and don't go into too many details. It seems like a lot of bloggers are more under the mentality that they want to publish posts often, but it doesn't really matter if they're super, super high quality, but that's kind of backward thinking in my opinion. That is just not a solid model for your blog and it's not going to create raving fans.

If you're just giving them a few details, you're not really giving them the whole story, and then it's not going to create these huge raving fans that love, love, love your website. Instead, give as much as possible. Don't write posts that barely scratch the surface on a topic. I'll say that again. Don't write posts that barely scratch the surface on a topic. Write posts that answer just about every question someone might have on a specific topic. You want to be detailed, you want to give the goods.

Think of it this way, write content worth selling. Write content that you could probably sell and make money from and then just give it away for free. You want to give, give, give so that when you do eventually want to sell something or you try to grow your audience, then your audience is already super engaged in what you're doing because you've given them so much awesome content already.

Again, don't be afraid to think differently. It is all good if you want to try something a little over the top. People are used to what they see in blog posts so shaking things up will help you standout. Try adding video, audio, or anything else that will level up your post. It's so, so, so okay if you haven't seen others in your niche do what you want to do. It's a good thing because you really want to stand out and it's hard to stand out if all you're doing are the same things that you see other people doing. So really try to think a little bit over the top, think a little bit differently, elaborate on what other people are doing and remind yourself that it's okay to be a little bit different.

Just to recap...

- Killer content includes a click worthy, descriptive title, great imagery and brand imagery.
- An easy-to-read structure-so remember we have our short paragraphs divided with easy to find and scan headings.
- A clear path of action, so ask yourself "what do you want somebody to do after they read this post?"
- An obvious takeaway, so ask yourself "what are they going to get out of the post?"
- Content that doesn't just brush the surface. Content that goes into detail, that gives them more facts, more information, that answers their questions before they ask them.

If you do all these things for every single post your blog is going to grow like a weed: uber fast in a good way (some weeds, like dandelions, are awesomely sweet). Killer content is the foundation of what you do with your blog. Then, once you create that killer content, and then on top of having a focus and a defined tribe, you'll get on Pinterest in the next chapters, and you're just going to blossom. It's going to grow really fast and your brand is going to grow and just be a lot more clearly defined and loved by your people. I'm very excited to get into the next chapters to show you some more.

CHAPTER FOUR

Pinterest Profile

In this chapter, we're going to be talking about mastering your Pinterest Profile because everyone wants to make a good first impression, right? That first impression is going to often dictate whether or not someone follows you and shares your pins.

Whenever you are using Pinterest, or really whenever you're using your blog or business in general, you should be asking yourself... "who am I attracting, or who am I trying to attract?" The point of it is that this is not about you; we're creating your entire brand, your entire blog or business for your tribe. This is not about you or your personal preferences or your interests or your hobbies; we're not using Pinterest for any of that. Don't be sad about that! Focusing on who you're trying to attract is going to bring you much bigger growth.

Step 1: become a business account...

Step 1 in creating a explosive Pinterest profile is to become a business account. A business account gives you access to Pinterest Analytics. We'll be talking about that later in a future chapter. If you want to switch to a business account, which I highly recommend even if you're not a business, is go to business.pinterest.com to switch to a business account.

Once you're established as a business account, you can also use the Pinterest Verify plugin for WordPress to upload a special code that they're going to give you on to your website. This makes it extra easy. Now if you have something else like Squarespace, no problem, you won't be able to use that specific plugin but you can still upload the code that they give you in to become a business account.

If you can't figure this out yourself, then just email Pinterest Support, and I've heard around the block that they will help you out. So why become a business account? Well, because you get access to some really cool features like analytics, promoted pins and rich pins. It's really in your best interest to become a business account even if you're not selling anything.

Step 2 : apply for rich pins...

Rich pins add your website name and your blog post title to

every single pin from your website. This creates awesome brand recognition where people see your blog pot title or your content title. They see your brand or blog name right below the pin and it just creates that kind of recognition where they see it in their feed and they start to recognize your name or your blog post title. You definitely want to get rich pins after you apply and get approved for a business account. This is just going to amplify your Pinterest account and help you start to rank higher in the Pinterest feed. It's totally worth it.

Step 3: create a killer profile...

Your profile should tell people what you do or how you help people, who exactly you serve. It should include a call to action to join your email list and you should include a photo or a logo. I know this is kind of a controversy so let me kind of break it down for you.

I believe that more often than not, you should be using a photo of your friendly old looking face. I want to see your pretty face. I want to be able to connect to a real human when I go to your Pinterest profile. You can use a logo if you are a bigger corporation, but unless you have a ton of employees and the business is really not about you at all, then you could use a logo. For most things like handmade businesses, blogs and businesses that don't have too many employees and really feature you as the owner, for example on your about page, I recommend using a photo instead. And lastly, you want to include keywords in your name.

Let's talk about the bio formula. I let you know that you want to include a few sentences in your actual bio on Pinterest and this is the formula I recommend using. You can start with "I help" or "I inspire", "I teach" – whatever kind of verb you want to use there. And then who do you help, so I help entrepreneurs, I help busy moms, I help lawyers – whoever you help. Do, become or learn, then what do you help them do, become or learn. So I help law students become lawyers. Basically, you're just showing people the kind of progression that you help them with. I help people who have no sense of style become fashionistas, so you can kind of see that progression there.

And then lastly, you want to include a call to action, like "Sign Up for My Free Seven Day Course" or "My Free Cheat Sheet". Give them some sort of incentive to sign up for your email list and then include a link where they can sign up. You can see this all in action on my own profile at pinterest.com/kerrielegend.

Just to recap...

Making an awesome first impression on Pinterest.

\\ First you want to get a business account and rich pins, yes even if you're not a business.

\\ You want to write a bio that tells people how you help them. \\ You should use a photo usually, but sometimes a logo.

\\ You want to have a call to action in your bio and you want to have keywords in your profile name because then it makes your profile searchable.

CHAPTER FIVE

Creating boards

Alrighty, now this is a big topic – creating boards. Think of your boards like categories on a blog. If you have a blog, then maybe you have different categories for the types of topics that you discuss on your blog. Think of your boards on Pinterest as your categories. This is basically asking the question, "what is your brand all about?" You're going to come up with some topics that your brand is all about and then morph those into your boards on Pinterest.

Conduct a board cleanse...

Strategy is the name of the game here when it comes to

board cleansing. Don't freak out - what I mean by that is delete or make secret any boards that aren't relevant to your target audience. Delete pins that are not evergreen or do not have relevance technology or application-wise anymore. You may have a Pinterest account already which is totally fine, but you might have some boards on your account that just aren't going to be relevant to that ideal audience that you're trying to attract. What I'm saying is either delete those boards or just turn them into secret boards so no one sees them.

Then once you do that, add any new boards that attract your target audience, and I'd aim for at least 15 to 20 boards in total. Of course, you can have more than that, but at the bare minimum, aim for 15 to 20. Now when I say that you want boards that attract your target audience, I'm saying think about those categories that you might put on your blog that would attract the right people to your website and then turn those categories into boards on Pinterest. So really, just think of the different general categories and topics that your target audience would be searching for and then create a board out of them.

Move your pins around...

If you want to move your pins when you are cleaning up your boards, maybe you have a board that has a few pins that are good and another board that has another few pins that are good and you just want to combine them into one board, you can move 50 pins at a time. If you go to one of your boards, you'll see this kind of four arrow symbol at the top. If you click that symbol then this second image will pop where it says "move", and then you can click the move button and then just click on any pin that you want to move to another board. This can make it much easier to clean up your pins because you can move up to 50 pins at one time.

Add targeted boards...

If you're having trouble coming up with new boards, maybe you've got 10 great board ideas but you don't really have any ideas for 5 to 10 more boards to add to your account, here is a little tip for you. On Pinterest, go into the little search bar at the top, type in some of your main keywords or things that your brand or business or blog are about, or the type of things that your target audience would be searching for, or any categories you already have.

Type any of those things into Pinterest search field and then this cool thing will pop up. You can see there is this row of all of these other keywords that someone might be searching for. Basically, Pinterest is giving you some ideas of different things that you could search for based on that keyword that you typed into the search field. So I searched "self-development", maybe you are a self-development blogger or maybe you are a therapist or something along those lines. I type that in there and then you see all of these different ideas and you can also toggle the arrows on the left or right side for even more ideas.

Based on this feedback, I could create another board called Mindset or Inspiration or Psychology. So I'm coming up with new ideas based on that one little seedling of an idea that I had before. If you're struggling to come up with multiple boards for your Pinterest profile, try this tip; I think you'll really enjoy it.

Now overall, your boards should only target topics that your ideal reader or customer would be searching for. So again, we're not creating personal boards, we're only creating things that our target audience would be searching for, and it should be within the realm of your niche. For example, maybe you target women who want to eat a healthy diet. So women who want to eat a healthy diet may also be interested in makeup, that might be something that some of them are interested in, but I wouldn't create a board called Makeup or Beauty because that's not really relevant to eating healthy. You see what I mean? So don't look for those loop holes where you kind of could add a board that maybe they would be interested in. You really want to keep it within the realm of your niche and that attracts the audience you want to serve.

Use straightforward board names...

Now for your board titles, use words that are straightforward, not flowery or poetic. I know that sometimes we have a tendency on Pinterest to create board titles that sound really unique because Pinterest is visual, it's creative, but it's also a search engine. You need to be straightforward with your naming conventions because otherwise your boards are not going to be searchable.

Think about the words that someone would be typing into Pinterest to search for something and then name your board that particular keyword or topic. Don't go too crazy here, just be as straightforward as you can. I know it might sound a little bit bland, but they're going to fall in love with your content and that's where the flowers and poetry live. It doesn't live in your keywords; it lives in the actual content that you are creating.

Fill up the boards...

Now it's time to fill your boards up with relevant content. I like to search for one topic at a time, so I just go up to the search field on Pinterest, type in a topic for that particular board and I go on a pinning spree. I just pin 50 or 100 things at one time if I'm starting a new board and I just fill it up with a lot of great content. So that way, I don't have to gradually fill it up over several months, I can just do it in one fell swoop.

Stay tuned for the Tailwind and BoardBooster tutorials in a future chapter because I'm going to be showing you how to schedule pins, so if you do go on a pinning spree like this, instead of pinning them all publicly at once, you can actually pin them so that they stagger and then go out over the span of a week or two.

Now a pro tip: if you're only following people who pin things that are relevant to your target audience, then your feed will have tons of content that you can quickly pin. So in this case, if you want to be a really fast pinner who wants to save a ton of time on Pinterest, I highly recommend unfollowing people who pin things that you personally like, but aren't relevant to your niche or your target audience, and then start to follow people in your niche who pin things that your target audience would like.

The reason for that is when you log into Pinterest, your Pinterest newsfeed with all those pins that you see, will only have content that you can pin to your brand's Pinterest account. That makes it very easy to find new content because every time you log in, you're going to be seeing a lot of new content from people in your niche or people that pin things that are relevant to the people you are trying to attract.

So you could just re-pin that content quickly and be done. Now I know some of you love using Pinterest and I don't blame you, it's a pretty awesome tool for personal use too, so if you want to keep following people that you love for your own personal use, you can absolutely do that too, just know that it might take you a little bit longer to find new stuff to pin to your boards or you could just create a new account solely for your personal use.

Just to recap...

- Do a board cleanse to clean up your account.
- Include at least 15 to 20 targeted boards.
- Use straightforward board titles, no poetry or flowery

language.
- Fill up your boards, so we're aiming to have at least 15 to 100 pins on every single board on your account.

I know that this is a big undertaking so if you can't do it right away, no problem. You have several weeks to be able to fit this into your schedule, but once you start doing this you'll start seeing your followers increase.

CHAPTER SIX

Pinterest branding strategy

Alright everybody, welcome back. In this chapter, we're talking about building a brand on Pinterest and really getting the juice out of that brand recognition.

Does it matter what you pin ?...

Does it matter what you pin? Yes. It does matter what you pin, because you don't just want to pin a bunch of random stuff. You should be pinning high-quality on-brand content. That's the key here; on-brand content. Remember, you are pinning for your audience, not yourself. So in this book, I'm not showing you how to create a beautiful, personal Pinterest with all of your random things that you are interested in. We are creating a Pinterest profile for a brand whether that brand is your blog, your business – whatever it may be, but we are creating this Pinterest for your audience. Now, you can still pin a lot of stuff that's interesting to you, but again, we're pinning for your audience, not for you. Let's get into it.

Building a strong brand...

A strong brand will help you stand out because it breeds consistency. People are going to start to recognize you and your work. Strong branding can consist of a lot of different things.

Your branding will be consistent if you stick to 3 to 5 complementary colors that you use on everything, not necessarily all at once. But you want to stick to these 3 to 5 complementary colors so that your branding looks very consistent and starts to stand out to people in their feed.

If they consistently see the same images or same style of images over and over again even though they are for a different post, people are going to start to take notice and get curious about those posts. So you want to stick to 3 to 5 complementary colors, and this works for everything in terms of your brand, not just on Pinterest, but definitely for your Pinterest images as well. And of course, you have the Pinterest handout for this book to help you discover some solid branding points.

Also, stick to two to three fonts only and always. I usually like to pick a font for headings, like headings, big fonts that you want to use, then subheadings, any font that you'll use for a sub-heading and then the text, text font. So 2 to 3 fonts only, sometimes your heading and subheading font will be the same and you only have two fonts. Avoid succumbing to the shiny object syndrome where you see a pretty font and decide to use it even though it has nothing to do with your branding. You've got to be consistent with your brand.

Your branding is consistent if you have a particular vibe or value to share, so not only do you know who you are but you know who you're not. I know that my brand is not like in your face punk rock, like cussing. I know that there's other brands out there that are more like that where they appeal to a different type of audience, but that's not my brand. It's important not only to know who your brand is but also who your brand is not.

Your brand is confusing if you see a new color, palette or new font and you just want to try it. That's okay in the beginning when you're testing out a lot of different things, maybe you're a new blogger, and honestly I think it is okay if you are brand-new because you can't really find what you love until you test out a lot of different things. But once you hit, let's say the six-month point, you should really create a more solid and consistent brand.

If you change your website's design or branding every month, you will confuse your audience. Now if this is a problem for you, if you really enjoy design, you really like switching up your blog design all the time, then hire someone to do it for you. You are much less likely to constantly renovate a brand that someone else created for you and that you paid for. Hire me to do your design – it's not overly expensive but it bites you just enough in the wallet while making you look amazing online all the while zapping your desire to change what I create for you.

Your brand is also confusing if you don't have a particular voice. Honestly, finding your voice with your brand just means that you found the confidence to write as yourself, that's it. I think a lot of people get confused about how to find their blogging voice, but really your voice is just talking as yourself, at your core.

Remember, create your brand around your tribe, not yourself. So create your branding around your tribe, not yourself. Again, this book about creating a popular blog and business, is not about creating something for you, we're throwing ourselves off the boat entirely. We are creating all of this stuff for our audience, our tribe.

Step 1: decide what you are an authority on...

Now this is going to be harder – if you want to grow your Pinterest profile, it is going to be harder to grow if you pin all the things. The same goes for your blog, your website, and your business. If you don't have that focus that you are the authority or the leader on something in particular, it's going to be a lot harder to grow. Just like with your blog, your Pinterest profile needs a focus, the same focus as your blog obviously, because you want to appeal to the same audience.

You can become an expert and authority in a certain niche.

You want to become an expert and an authority in a certain niche, not just spreading yourself too thin and touching surface on 10 topics, but picking one topic that you are a leader in. And the content you pin should fall into this niche. Again, everything is very consistent, your brand is obvious and on point. Of course, asking yourself the questions, who are you pinning for, who is your tribe, who is your audience, and deciding who that person is, what you can pin for them and become a leader for that person, will drive your blog and Pinterest profile that much further.

Can you pin other stuff? If you are pinning for your tribe, can you pin stuff that isn't totally irrelevant to that first topic? It is important to become an authority on a certain topic, this is what is going to help you stand out, but you can still pin other things occasionally, just make sure that they are on brand for your audience. I share a lot of blogging tips, entrepreneur tips, social media tips, so honestly, I do not ever pin a recipe. I just don't. It's not part of my brand model at the moment, and may never be.

Everything should still tie together for that ideal audience member, should still be very cohesive to your brand. But if they are too off brand or too random, then create secret boards so you can see them but others can't, so if there is just a recipe that you are dying to make then just pin it to a secret board. Don't worry, you can still use Pinterest to its full potential. You don't need to just throw everything away, but just create secret boards to keep those things for yourself that you don't want your audience to see.

Step 2: create a consistent aesthetic...

You'll probably see that on my own kerrielegend.com board that my pins all kind of look the same, don't they? When people see my pins in their feed, they immediately recognize them as something they've either seen before or if they've been to my website, then they know that it is my pin. All my pins are branded in some way.

Now, you want to create your own visually consistent pins for that same reason, to build brand recognition. If your blog is full of color, joy and happiness, then you want to create images that are colorful and happy too, because again, it gives you that brand consistency. If you create products that have a certain aesthetic to them, you want to pin images that have that aesthetic quality to them as well, because again, you are creating a brand on Pinterest and people aren't just going to follow you for your content, they're going to follow you for everything else that you are pinning too, so you really need to think of your pinning strategy in this kind of holistic sense. Think of it this way, you want people to associate you with a certain aesthetic.

Just to recap...

- Decide which topics are at the core of your brand,

what are you going to be pinning about, and who are you trying to attract. You should be answering those questions every time you pin something to your account.

- Decide on your aesthetic style, so what kind of pins are you going to be sharing, do you have some sort of style that you're going to stick to, is that important to your audience.

Fill out the handouts for best results and consistency. The handouts have some targeted activities that are going to help you really create this brand consistency on Pinterest.

CHAPTER SEVEN

Designing the perfect pin

Whether you consider yourself a designer or not, I'm going to show you how to design share-worthy pins, so the things that go into great pins, and a simple strategy for creating beautiful pins even if you've never touched a piece of design software. Are you ready for this? Let's do it.

The perfect pin checklist...

The perfect pin checklist includes:
1. It should be vertical – I recommend roughly 800 x 1200 pixels. You can kind of skew this a little bit, but

the general concept is you want your pin to be tall rather than wide and horizontal. The reason for this is because vertical pins just appear larger in the Pinterest feed. You want your pins to appear larger because then they are more likely to be seen, which means they are more likely to get re-pins and click throughs to your website.

2. Use on brand colors and fonts – we've talked about brand consistency before and it is so important. When I started my blog, I fell in love with a new font pretty much every week – it's hard as a designer to stick with a brand and now show off all your millions of fonts (believe me – so hard!). All of my Pinterest images and blog post images looked completely different week after week. As a graphic designer, it's SOOOO tempting to try out new fonts and use them everywhere. Trust me – it's practically unbearable. But for consistency, I have to stick with the fonts that I have chosen. Eventually, I realized that people were not able to recognize my blog. I was dazzling them with color and fonts and layouts galore. It was like every time you met up with a friend and then they change everything about their appearance and you are like, "Wait, I thought you looked different last week." This is how people are feeling about your website and your branding if you're constantly

LEARN PINTEREST STRATEGY

changing your hairstyle online, if you know what I mean. The solution to that is choosing a few fonts and a few colors and sticking with those throughout everything that you create for your brand.

3. Include large easy to read text – use a bit of text along with a great image. Including some text on your image to let people know what they're going to get out of clicking through to your post or product.

4. Include your website link –I've seen people who put a giant logo on their pin or they put their website link super huge somewhere on their pin, which I understand, you are excited about your blog or your business. It totally makes sense and I'm sure I did the same thing too, but the fact of the matter is that people on Pinterest don't yet care about you, and I say that very lovingly, but you have to get people to care about you by getting them over to your website and seeing how awesome your products or your blog posts are, but for the time being, they don't really care too much about you or your logo or your website name. For now, it's just there to kind of build that brand recognition in a small way and to kind of copyright your images to make sure that no one rips them off of Facebook. We want to use that website link in case your pin ends up somewhere else in the Internet universe, but we don't want it to be the focal

point. We really want your headline to be the focal point of your pin.

5. Include a screenshot of your incentive – If you are using opt-in incentives or content upgrades which we're going to be talking about more in a later section, then I highly recommend including a little screenshot of your incentive on your pin itself and then something that lets people know what they're going to get for free. I don't just say free workbook without a screenshot because I feel that when people see the actual workbook, they are more likely to want it because they can visualize it on their computer or in their hands, because they can actually see what it looks like. It's more powerful to have an image of that freebie that they're going to get and you can just put that right on top of your Pinterest image.

6. Save your files using keywords – Now you can't really see this one inside of this image here, but when you are saving your image onto your computer and then uploading it to your website, you want to use some keywords in the file name. If you're just uploading something from your camera, then it might sound something like CYX_542.jpeg which is not really searchable unless you're searching for something called CYX_542, which is probably not the case. So in this case, every time you create a blog post, title your

image that you're going to pin on to Pinterest with a keyword. Whatever the topic of your blog post is, or whatever kind of product you are going to be pinning, make sure that you save it as something that's relevant. I might save it as something like blogging-tips. If you are creating a meal plan, you might save it as paleomealplan.jpeg. You just want to name it with some keywords in the file name so that your image is a little bit more searchable.

7. Use evergreen content – the best content on Pinterest is evergreen content. I'm going to explain a little bit more about that in just a second, but keep that word, evergreen, in your mind for now. Now all the pins on Pinterest have the same width so you can imagine a horizontal pin with the same width as a vertical pin, it's just going to look a lot smaller. That's why you want to use vertical pins. Now, back to evergreen content, which I briefed you on in a past chapter. Of course you want to use evergreen content. Evergreen content is essentially just content that is timeless. It's as useful today as it will be in one year, so it is not time sensitive like a pin for an event or a webinar or something along those lines. Think of timeless evergreen content that you can create and then pin that on to Pinterest. Now Pro tip: if you are new, maybe you don't have a lot of content yet,

maybe you are a new business owner, a new blogger and you just don't have a lot of things to pin yet. If that's the case, what I recommend doing is creating multiple pin templates for each blog post or each product that you have and then pin them all. So instead of just creating one template for that blog post, you can create three templates, so now if you have 10 blog posts and each one has three different images that are great for Pinterest inside of it, then that's essentially 30 things that you can pin on to Pinterest even though you only have 10 blog posts or 10 products. This is also a good way to A/B test your pins or your headlines. You can create similar templates. Now, here's a disclosure. I have over 100+ templates just for Pinterest that I can use, and I make them available on my website for purchase if you want them (they're amazing.) You want to again, stay on brand with the same fonts and colors, but maybe just change the layout or something or change the text or the headline and then test it. Layout changes are perfectly acceptable within your brand. You're not violating any image rules there. You can try different wording or different phrasing or different layout for your pin and then see which one gets more re-pins, and then you'll have a good idea of which one you should continue using in the future.

LEARN PINTEREST STRATEGY

More design tips...

If you're not a designer, maybe you are struggling to create on-brand pin templates or any kind of designs for your website, so try this easy pin design. Put a transparent layer on top of a photo, so you can do this very easily in Photoshop (you can get a month of it for FREE). You basically just put a slab of color on top of a photo and then just fiddle with the opacity a little bit so that it's not a completely opaque image but you can see the photo behind it. Then just add some text on top of that and voila! You have created a stellar Pinterest image.

Of course, you may want to add some other things that we talked about earlier like your website name down at the bottom, but in general, you can create something that looks like this and it looks great, it will work extraordinarily well on Pinterest. It doesn't have to be super crazily designed. You don't have to do anything too complex. Although, beautifully, well-thought-out pins using unique layouts perform even better. Be sure to check them out on my website and change up your game to a whole new level.

You can create beautiful images in a really simple way. Again, just put that transparent layer on top, and you might want to use a color that goes with your branding and then just pop some text on top and you're good to go. For some design program recommendations, I recommend Photoshop for beginners. They have a free plan available. They also have a paid plan. I do not recommend apps like Canva because all the "good" images you have to pay for, and when you're on a budget, it's very tempting to "settle" for second best. The point is to impress people – so unless you're willing to spend $1+ per image, I would recommend other options. For people who want to get more design experience or who already have some design experience, I still recommend Photoshop. Photoshop is around $19 a month, so not too bad there.

Just to recap...

- Create pins that follow the rules of perfect pins that we went over.
- Create multiple pin images for each post if you don't have a lot of content yet.

CHAPTER EIGHT

How To Use This Template

This chapter we're going to discuss how to master the Smart Feed on Pinterest and also what the heck the Smart Feed is. If you really want to get awesome results on Pinterest then this section is for you.

The Pinterest Smart Feed...

It was introduced in late 2014 so it hasn't been around for a super long time. Pinterest used to display pins as newest first, now it displays them as best first, very much like a search engine would. You might have been worried that you could pin too many things and bother your followers, because if you're pinning 30 things at once, then when it displayed your pins as newest first, then all 30 pins would be displayed all at once. Now because of the Smart Feed, it displays them as best first. It basically ranks all of the pins that people share. If your pins are not best first, then you know what happens? They are not getting seen.

It judges each user with an internal ranking system to determine whose pins are the best. Bottom line, if Pinterest does not rank you highly, your pins won't be seen right away and sometimes not at all, so that kind of sucks if your pins are not getting seen by your followers. The Smart Feed has totally changed the game, but I am confident that I have cracked the code and I'm about to share it with you.

I just want to reiterate the fact that Pinterest is a search engine. So if you think about Google, Google has algorithms, really sophisticated algorithms where it is scanning all of the information out there to find the very best articles to rank first in its search engine. When you type in "taco recipe" on Google, it's finding you the best taco recipes, and it takes a lot of factors into consideration like who the site is, whether there are pictures, videos, how long the post is. There are a lot of different factors that go into Google's ranking system.

Now Pinterest has started implementing a similar ranking system where they don't want their users to just pull up random things that aren't very relevant or aren't very useful. They want people who use Pinterest to love Pinterest, so they internally created what is referred to as "user voice", which is part of their algorithm.

There are users who are not going to love Pinterest; they are casual users who are just looking for things to read and pin. They're not going to love Pinterest if every time they click through to an article, it's not very good, so that's why Pinterest has implemented this best first algorithm, much like a search engine like Google would. They are displaying pins as best first.

Now, if you remember only one thing from this book, remember this. Pinterest is a search engine not a social media platform. So like Google, it has an algorithm that ranks content from best and most relevant to its users, to irrelevant or weak content. If you're not incorporating SEO or search engine functionality onto your Pinterest account and with your pins and boards etc., then your pins are not going to be showing up at the top of people's feeds. They're going to be shoved at the bottom or maybe just not even seen. Ever.

Following the steps to outsmart the Smart Feed gives you the best shot at showing up at the top of people's feeds. The cornerstone of search engines is keywords, so we're going to be talking about keywords and how to implement them into your Pinterest account so that you can again the best results possible on Pinterest by using it as a search engine, not a social media platform.

A few Smart Feed factors...

It's all about high-quality content. Everything in the Smart Feed revolves around high-quality content. That's basically the key to getting your content to rank higher. There are a few things that go into that as well.

Pins with more re-pins are assumed to be better. Pinterest isn't exactly reading all the articles out there. That would take forever. They are not ranking them hand by hand, one by one, but they look at a few different factors to see which pins appear to be the best. Pins with more re-pins are assumed to be better, and more high-quality, because it shows that people like those pins. Pins with descriptions are more easily found and shared.

So again, Pinterest is a search engine, so if you don't have a description on your pin, people are not going to be finding it as easily. If they can't find it, they can't re-pin it. Pinners who share consistently are ranked higher. People who are constantly pinning on Pinterest are assumed by Pinterest to be more high-quality pinners because they are in it to win it. Pins that lead to relevant links are better. Pinterest doesn't want its users to be clicking a bunch of links and have it lead to random websites or suspicious websites or broken links. They want it to lead to relevant links that the actual article that it says it's linking to. Relevant links are better.

Mastering the Smart Feed...

Now let's master this smart feed, step-by-step. There are a few different ways, that we can go through it. Make sure that your pins are being seen in the Smart Feed and this will grow your account as well. If you are not doing these things, then I've got to tell you that your account is probably demoted in Pinterest's internal ranking system which is why it might be harder for your account to grow, why you might not be seeing as many re-pins on your pins or on your account. So factoring in the Smart Feed algorithm is really going to help you grow your account and your website.

Step 1 : clean up your old pins...

Let's do some spring cleaning. Delete any pins that are off-brand or irrelevant to your audience. This isn't necessarily part of the Smart Feed, but because of some things that we're going to be doing later on in this book, it is important that all of your pins are on point. So if you wouldn't pin it nowadays, delete it.

Now again, some later strategies involve re-pinning your old content, so we want to make sure your content is worth re-pinning. Now when I did this, going through my old pins, I found a lot of stuff where I was like "I pinned that? Like, why did I pin that?" I no longer share pins on "How to start a blog". My audience has moved way beyond that. My audience is there to dominate and succeed and already have blogging figured out.

You want to go through old pins on your boards and this is going to take a while, and just delete anything that's really off-brand, irrelevant or visually unappealing. Anything that just doesn't work, something that you wouldn't pin now, delete it. I

LEARN PINTEREST STRATEGY

would also kind of take a little bit of caution, I wouldn't go through and delete 1000 pins in one day because Pinterest might think what's happening to their account; is this spam, is this person a real person. They might flag your account if you go through and delete 1000 pins in one day. I recommend sticking to 100, 200 per day deleting your off-brand pins. No more than 100 to 200 per day and you should be totally fine.

Step 2 : delete pins with bad, broken links...

If your pins lead to broken or irrelevant links, meaning it's leading to a website that has nothing to do with the pin itself, then this is going to lower your internal user ranking with Pinterest. Pinterest is looking for the highest quality pins and users to share.

Think of Pinterest, again, as you would Google. So when you type a search term on Google, you're not going to get irrelevant results. You're generally going to get the best content on the Internet that has to do with the thing that you typed into Google. Pinterest is becoming more like Google, so they want to only share the best content, too. If your boards are filled with pins that lead to irrelevant websites or that have broken links, then it's going to kind of demote your profile and make it so that your pins and your own content get demoted as well.

Pin Doctor is a pretty cool tool on BoardBooster. It will search all of your bad links, broken links, irrelevant links, duplicate pins etc., and it only costs one cent per pin to search for those, so super worth it. It basically just crawls your account and then finds any pin that it deems as irrelevant or unworthy of being on your account so that you can easily and quickly delete them.

Step 3 : add pin descriptions...

Great images get people to re-pin the image, but great descriptions get people to click through to your website. This is also an opportunity for you to be a "related pin" or a "picked for you". If you've been around the Pinterest block for a little while, then you've probably seen in your feed, related pins or picked for you pins. They are labelled that way in your feed.

Basically, Pinterest is selecting pins that it thinks you will enjoy based on the other kinds of content you pin. **You could become that pin for someone else which is the whole point here**, but they're not going to find your pin unless you have **pin descriptions with keywords** in them. We're going to be talking about that a little bit more, but get that idea in your head that you have a big opportunity here to get in front of more people.

Now a trick for adding descriptions. You might have had the problem before where you weren't able to add a description, like there is a random description that's automatically added to your photos or your images from your website. If you are using WordPress, you can write a description that gets added to your images every time someone pins them. Even if some random person comes to your site, uses the pin it button and pins your image, that description that you wrote with those keywords and that call to action is going to be automatically embedded into the pin. This is pretty awesome.

You just add the description as the image's Alt text before you insert the image into the post. It doesn't work if you've already inserted the image, you need to go back, delete the image, reinsert it or add the Alt text and then reinsert it into the post, and then you're always going to have that description when somebody, anybody pins from your site. So now every pin from your site will have a description rather than like cute-summer-dress.jpeg or the post title or something that's totally irrelevant.

Step 4 : get people to pin your content...

The first person who should be pinning your content is you. You want to pin your own content first which honestly I thought was the weirdest thing when I first started doing it. I felt like I was self-promoting and just being a big Pinterest weirdo by pinning my own content, but you **should** be pinning your own content. You don't want to solely rely on other people to do it for you.

Second, add a pin it button to your website. The one that I recommend for WordPress users is jQuery Pin It button for Images, but whether you are on WordPress or Squarespace or any kind of website, you can use a plug-in to add a pin it button to your website which makes it really easy for people to pin your images for you.

You can also promote your pins in certain Facebook groups. Be careful because you don't want to spam in a Facebook group that doesn't allow these types of promotions, but there are some Facebook groups that you can seek out that are specifically for sharing your Pinterest images and getting people to re-pin them. You might want to search for some of those Facebook groups to help some of your pins gain traction quickly.

You also may want to add a Pinterest widget to your relevant blog posts and your sidebar. A Pinterest widget is basically this little Pinterest box that you can add inside of your blog content or on your sidebar, or anywhere on your website and it shows your Pinterest board with your pins and it has a follow button so people can see the types of content that you pin and they can also follow your Pinterest account.

Let's say you have a blog post that you wrote about healthy eating, how to eat healthier and you have a board on Pinterest called "Healthy Eating". It would be perfect to embed that Pinterest board widget into your blog post and tell people "if you really enjoy this blog post, why don't you follow me on Pinterest?" It makes a sense, so that is another option for you to use as well. Now you can add a Pinterest widget by simply going to one of your boards on your Pinterest account and there's just a little button you can select to grab that code for the Pinterest widget and place it on your website. And lastly, you want to add keyword rich descriptions to all of your pins on Pinterest. We're going to be talking more about this, but I want to reiterate it because it's a huge point in this book.

Why is it so important to get people pinning your content? Well, Pinterest has something now called Aggregate Re-Pin Numbers, which means the pins show the total number of re-pins among all Pinterest users, rather than just a number of re-pins that that particular user received.

Now this is a good thing because before, your pins would be scattered around people's profiles and most of the time, they would only have one or two pins. They just have a handful of pins really, because those users weren't getting a lot of repins on your content or any content, but not because they have these aggregate pin numbers which show the total re-pins, they look pretty beefed up which adds a whole lot of social proof, meaning when someone sees this pin that says 2.4 thousand re-pins, they immediately think, "That sounds like a pretty good article, maybe I should read it. It seems like a lot of other people are interested in it. I want to re-pin it!" These are the thoughts that people are having, but if they saw this pin and it only had two re-pins, they might not really have that same reaction.

Having these total re-pin counts on your pins does give it an element of social proof which is why you should encourage all of your followers to pin your content. Every single pin counts at this point because it all goes towards that total re-pin number rather than just having those scattered one or two re-pins on your followers' different accounts.

Step 5: be consistent...

The Smart Feed rewards users who pin consistently and often, so you want to be consistent on Pinterest. It's important to pin between 50 and 100 pins per day which I know sounds insane, but don't worry because I'm going to show you how to loop pins with BoardBooster so that this will literally take you about 30 minutes per week. Or, you can use Tailwind to schedule. I'm not kidding.

Now, I cannot stress enough how important these steps are. This is what will help you become a high-quality pinner stat. We really want Pinterest to realize that you are a high-quality user, that you care about Pinterest, and that you are sharing awesome information. But if you're not following the steps in this section, then it's going to be hard for Pinterest to rank you highly in their feed. I can't stress enough how important these steps are.

Just to recap...

- The Smart Feed is Pinterest's algorithm that you can outsmart.
- You want to clean up your old pins, add pin and board descriptions and be a consistent pinner if you want to see great results on Pinterest.

CHAPTER NINE

Search Engine Optimization

Now let's talk about adding SEO to your pins and boards. So what exactly is SEO? What does this stand for? It stands for Search Engine Optimization which means that it helps your content appear at the top of the feed or search results. The same thing goes for Google. So the post that you see at the top of Google search results whenever you search for something, typically have strong SEO. In this section, I'm going to show you how to get stronger SEO on Pinterest. A major component of SEO is using relevant keywords that your target audience is searching for, so keep that in mind as we talk about SEO.

Your profile name which we talked about in one of the earlier sections, your pin descriptions and your board descriptions, and bonus, you should also be using it off of Pinterest inside of your content and with your content's title on your actual website. So you've got a few different places that you should be using keywords and the more that you pump up the keywords in these different locations, the better results you are going to get on Pinterest. It's really that simple.

Starting off with your profile name, you can see that in my profile I put my actual name, but then I put a little column and then I wrote some keywords. These are keywords that are designed to attract the people that I serve. I want you to add keywords to your profile name on Pinterest as well. This is going to make your profile more searchable, and it has another effect because now when people see your profile, they're going to see those keywords right up front and center as soon as they get to your profile. This is a good thing because the people who should be on your profile, your target audience that you are trying to attract. If they see those keywords, they are immediately going to resonate with them and they are going to feel like, "Oh I found an incredible account that I really love that gets me." It's going to repel the people who aren't right for you, which is an equally good thing because the worst thing you can do is grow a big audience full of people who don't give a crap about your brand. We can simultaneously attract the right people and repel the wrong people by simply adding keywords to your profile name.

Now step two is to add keywords to your pin descriptions. Pinterest has limited your descriptions to only about 50 characters. You can see here that my pin description actually gets cut off a little bit and this is all I can really fit on my pin. You want to add keywords to your description. You don't really have a whole lot of room so you can't really write sentences or anything like that, but you can add some words that people might be searching for in order to find that particular pin.

So think about what would your target audience be searching for in order to find this pin and how can you add some keywords to your pin's description to lead those people to that pin. Now you may also want to consider which keywords you want to rank for. For example, if you're a real estate agent in Atlanta, then you're probably pretty location dependent. You're not going to be helping people find houses in New York City because you live in Atlanta and you probably help people in the real estate market where you live.

In that case, you probably want to rank for keywords like real estate agent Atlanta, so I would add those keywords to every single pin of yours that you share on Pinterest. Now that's just one example. You may want to rank for pins for a variety of reasons, maybe you sell a product or maybe your blog is very specific on a certain topic so you want to rank for those specific keywords. You can add the same keywords to all of your pins in order to really build up that momentum with those keywords for your content. Remember, be straightforward. No flowery language here my friends. Your keywords should be very straightforward, to the point. For example, if you sell Bohemian jewelry, try keywords like "handmade jewelry, Bohemian jewelry or Bohemian style", because all of these are things that people might be searching for on Pinterest and they are designed to attract your target customers, or maybe you are a graphic designer. Try keywords like "graphic design, logo design or feminine website". Again, these are the types of things that people might be searching for in order to find a graphic designer, maybe they're looking for someone to design their website for them. So they would be typing different things like this into Pinterest. Maybe you blog about getting out of debt, so you could try keywords like "how to get out of debt, financial tips or how to save money". Again, these are the types of things that people would be typing into Pinterest's search bar in order to find your content or your products.

Lastly, you want to add keywords to your board descriptions. It is no mistake that this particular board on my account is my most popular board. This board tends to get the most re-pins, the most impressions and the most followers because look at all those keywords. I've got a bunch of keywords to attract people to this board, so if they are searching for these keywords on Pinterest or sometimes even on Google, they will find this board. It's a great way to attract people to your pins, your boards and your profile by simply adding keywords that they would be searching for anyways.

Now just like your pins, you want your boards to have keyword rich descriptions. I would brainstorm 10 to 15 keywords or phrases and add them to your board descriptions. This is again going to help your boards pop up in search results or be that coveted "picked for you" board. "Picked for you" is basically when Pinterest picks your board and puts it into somebody's Pinterest feed. They don't have to be following you because Pinterest selected your board out of all the other boards because you've got rocking SEO and they can tell, so they are going to put you in other people's Pinterest feeds which is going to increase the likelihood that people are going to follow that board or re-pin the content from that board. This is a very big deal and another reason why you want to add keywords to your board descriptions because otherwise, maybe Pinterest won't know what that board is about. And lastly, Pinterest boards can actually pop up in Google's search results. Not only will you be able to pop up in Pinterest search results, but you will be able to pop up on Google too if you have good Pinterest SEO, so killing two birds with one stone here my friends.

Now altogether: adding keywords to your profile name, your pin descriptions and board descriptions makes your account and content searchable which is huge, because without keywords no one will find your content. Think about that for a second because most Pinterest users do not do this, most Pinterest users do not do this, most Pinterest users don't even know that this is a strategy.

By adding keywords to your pins and boards and profile name, you are immediately jumping ahead of majority of Pinterest users out there. This ends up resulting in huge gains and quick wins against other Pinterest users. After filling your account with keywords, you're going to begin to shoot up to the top of people's feeds which means more followers on Pinterest, more traffic to your website and more email subscribers.

Just to recap...

- Your Pinterest growth relies heavily on SEO and keywords
- You want to use keywords in your profile name, your pin descriptions and your board descriptions
- Put it all together and this will help your content to be found and shared on autopilot and like crazy

CHAPTER TEN

Group Boards

In this chapter, we're talking about group boards, your new secret weapon. But first, what is a group board?

What is a group board ?...

So someone owns the board, the group board and invites other people to pin to it. They are the owner of the board, they created it and then they can invite people to pin to that board. So some group boards have two people pinning to it and some have 200. It really depends on the board, but somebody owns it and then they invite other people to pin to it. Any pin shared to that board are shown to anyone following it, so not necessarily your followers. So the pins that are shared on that board are only shown to the people who are following that group board, so not people who are following your Pinterest account.

Why group boards ?...

Why do we like them? They allow you to get your content in front of new people. So again, if you have say 300 followers, but you are joining a group board which has 3,000 followers, then your pins are going to be shared with 3,000 people, not just your 300 people.

That's awesome, right? If you join a group board that has a lot more followers than you, then you are basically increasing your number of followers without having to increase your number of followers. It's pretty awesome.

Group boards are going to increase your traffic and your re-pins. And they will also show others that you are a leader and authority in your niche. I always tell people to join group boards that are specific to their niche.

For my business, I wouldn't join a group board for recipes because that's so irrelevant to the content that I create. Even if I could get a lot of click-throughs to my website or something, I wouldn't do that. You want to join group boards that are very relevant to your niche, and it's going to set you apart because you are constantly pinning to all of these different group boards in your niche. You are getting in front of different audiences and different followers. Now they are not the end-all, be-all, but they are helpful to growing your Pinterest profile and driving traffic (for free!) to your blog and business.

Step 1 : finding relevant group boards...

Option one is to search for a specific keyword on Pinterest and then filter by boards. You want to look for boards with multiple pinners, and you might have to click through to different boards to see if there are multiple pinners on that board.

Unfortunately, Pinterest makes it a little bit difficult for you to figure out if it's a group board or not, but luckily, there is a website, called pingroupie.com, which allows for you to search for a specific keyword just as you would on Pinterest, but it shows you only group boards from that topic. You can go through pingroupie.com and find boards on a topic that fits your niche and attracts the target audience you are trying to reach. It also has good engagement. So then you can click through from pingroupie to those boards and then request to join them. That's a little bit easier.

Now a quick tip is if there are pinners that you love that are in your niche, that attract the people that you want to reach, go to their profile on Pinterest to see which group boards they are a part of. You can see if you go to someone's profile, you can see a group board is indicated by the little two-person icon. Look for that on these Pinterest profiles to see if any of the people you admire or have an audience you want to reach if they are part of any group boards and then you can request to join those group boards because they are probably working well for that person if they are part of that group board if they are seeing success.

Step 2 : selecting the best group boards...

So again, you don't want to join just any group board, you want to join the best ones, and joining 30 group boards is going to look spammy because these group boards are also going to be on your profile. I would recommend putting them at the bottom of your profile because they are not your board unless you own the group board, but they are not your boards so you don't want them to be the first thing that somebody sees when they come to your account.

I always put them at the bottom, but having 30 or even 10 kind of looks spammy, so at most aim to join five excellent boards. Now here is what the best boards have in common, and this is what I want you to look for when you are either on pingroupie or you are searching for boards on Pinterest to join:

- They are frequently pinned to. This is probably the most important thing because you want other people to be constantly pinning to these boards because if they are not, it means that you can't pin them consistently. You hopefully want people to be pinning to these boards all throughout the day so that you can pin to the board every day and it doesn't look spammy because if you are pinning every day and nobody else is pinning, then it's all going to be the stuff that you've pinned and that's going to look kind of spammy and just not very good. So you want it to be frequently pinned on so that it's easier for you to share your content on those boards without looking spammy.

- Pins on the best boards have an average of three or more re-pins. If you check out a group board and you notice that most of the pins have like one re-pin, zero re-pins, then it is probably not worth your time because this group board is not getting very much traction. You really want to look for group boards that have an average of three or more re- pins. I say average because some of them might have one re-pin or zero re-pins, but then others will have five or seven or ten, so on average, you want to have three or more re-pins, ideally, even five or more, but let's say three or more just to give them the benefit of the doubt.

- Pinners share quality content on the best boards. If you go through these best boards and it just looks like spammy, buy my product, visit my blog kind of stuff, then you know that it is not quality content. You want to look for group boards where people are sharing a mix of other people's content and their own content, and they are really searching for that high-quality content to share, because group boards are not immune to the smart feed. They need to have quality content as well to really pop up in the smart feed too. You want other people to be sharing quality content, and that's also going to show you that the people who are following that group board are quality followers because quality followers are not going to be following spammy group boards. So you want to make sure the other pinners share quality content. Also, you want to make sure the board is highly relevant to your main niche and the core of your brand. So again, just going back to your focus and choosing group boards based on your main focus or topic.

Now you can also use your Pinterest Analytics which we are going to get into in a later section, but you can use your Pinterest Analytics with group boards. If we go to your Pinterest profile, you can see that highlighted at the top, and then we take a look at impressions and scroll down, you're going to see a section like this that says boards with top impressions. Now this is going to show you which group boards you joined that are giving you the best benefit.

Step 3 : creating a schedule...

LEARN PINTEREST STRATEGY

I pin all my content to my own boards first. I pin all the stuff from my blog to my own boards, typically my brand board so I pin there first. From there, I re-pin my content to my group boards at a 1:1 ratio.

For each pin of mine that I pin to a group board, I pin one of somebody else's too. You don't just want to go to a group board and pin only your own stuff, that's going to look spammy and it's just not really cool. You want to make sure that you are pinning other people's stuff too.

Now check your group boards every day to see if you can pin to them, so multiple times a day if they are particularly active. Again, that's why it is important group boards are pinned to frequently because you want to be able to pin to them frequently too. The more often people are pinning to them, the more often you can pin to them without looking as spammy.

Now I don't share more than three pins at a time because again, you don't want to look spammy. I can share a couple of mine and one of somebody else's and call it a day. Now if this sounds like a lot of work, checking your group boards every day, I know that that can sound like a lot of work, stay tuned for the next section because you can schedule all of this. There is a way that I'm going to show you how to do this where you don't even have to schedule it, it just – it's basically automatic, takes me like 30 minutes a week to do all of my Pinterest scheduling, 100 pins a day – it's crazy. But good.

Just to recap...

- Group boards can get your pins in front of much larger audiences, so if you have a small audience and you join a group board with a big audience, you can get your pins in front of much more followers.
- It is important to find relevant group boards with a high re-pin rate and lots of activity.
- Use your Pinterest Analytics to see which group boards are delivering the best results and you can also see which ones are delivering the worst results so that you can remove the boards that are not doing well. So if you are part of some boards that are giving you the lowest amount of impressions or re-pins, then you know that you can leave those boards because they are just not really helping you. Now go to pingroupie.com or go to Pinterest and search for some keywords to try and find some group boards that are going to be awesome and help you reach a larger audience.

CHAPTER ELEVEN

Scheduling and Looping Pins

In this chapter, we're going to be talking about scheduling and looping your pins using my favorite Pinterest scheduler, Tailwind, and looping them with BoardBooster. The BoardBooster program helps me make 100 re-pins of my choosing every single day. I schedule with Tailwind because I can see the pins and the times they'll be scheduled, and also check a ton of analytics. Each program offers something different.

Rumor has it that Tailwind is going to be adding the looping feature (as of the date of this book's publishing) so if they do that, I will probably go exclusive with Tailwind, because I enjoy the interface that much more. BoardBooster has a more archaic feel to it, in my opinion, which makes the user experience a bit less enjoyable. It's the looping feature in BoardBooster that is the game changer.

Plus, Tailwind has a tribe feature that I have found beneficial in getting my pins shared, which is a huge plus. Right now, as of the date of publication, Tailwind is still in alpha development with the tribe feature, but it is fully functional and it works great.

BoardBooster can schedule pins for you, and you can specify pins of your choosing because it's not like they are selecting all of these pins for you; you get to choose them, and make sure that they are on-brand, make sure that they are relevant to your audience and then it will re-pin them for you every single day. What I did find with BoardBooster in using their pin finder feature was a lot of non-relevant content which took additional time to vet out. I'm a busy gal, so I stuck with Tailwind because I could just pin from my tribes and search for relevant content within that area.

Now using Tailwind and BoardBooster combined, I grew my following to over 2000 Pinterest followers in two months and it's continuing to grow right now at a rate of about 100 to 200 followers per month.

At the moment, my account is growing at about 10 followers per day, I really want you to see that same success and that's why I am sharing Tailwind and BoardBooster with you because it's a really awesome program. My page views have doubled, and with my Pinterest following growing with the number of re-pins that I'm making growing, my visitor and page counts have doubled as well, and my email list is starting to surge even more.

I only need to use Pinterest for about 30 minutes per week. So you might be thinking like wow, that's a lot of results but is it going to take me forever? And honestly, I'm using Pinterest a lot less time-wise than when I was using before, so it's incredible how time-saving it is and how effective it is. I'm all about finding things that are time-saving and effective.

Get this, it only costs me $15 per month for Tailwind and around $10 for BoardBooster. I don't know if $25 per month is cost prohibitive to you. Hopefully since you're in this book that will be an expense that you can manage, but even if you can't, there are different plans so you could start at even five dollars per month. Use my codes and invites at the front of the book so you can get moving without any expense incurred straight away.

Scheduling with Tailwind or BoardBooster

Remember that first function we talked about, scheduling. So instead of pinning all your pins at once, you can schedule them to be pinned later on. Remember – I primarily use Tailwind for my scheduling. But in BoardBooster, you create secret feeder boards where your pins are saved and pinned out. It will just be for every board that you have that's public, it will create a secret board for that board. So you just pin your scheduled pins onto the secret feeder board and then BoardBooster will abide by the schedule that you create. You create the schedule in BoardBooster and it will send out those secret pins to your public boards during the rotation that you set. It's very easy to use, it might sound kind of complex, but trust me, it's super easy.

Looping boards...

My absolute favorite feature. It's going to re-pin your content from your boards, starting with the oldest content first. This is awesome because it gives new life to your old pins. Remember those pins that are just sitting there? It also increases re-pin rate as your following grows. If you have 200 followers right now and then as you start implementing all these strategies from this book, maybe you grow to 1000 followers. Those pins that you shared when you had 200 followers probably don't have as many re-pins because you didn't have as big of an audience to share them to.

As your audience grows, you can use this looping feature to re-pin those old pins and now all those thousand people or thousand followers are going to see your pins again, re-pin them. Then it also has this cool feature, so after X amount of days it deletes the pin with the lower amount of re-pins. You can imagine with looping where it's repinning your old content, you're going to have two of the same pin on one board. Now you might think, like are people going to notice or is it going to be obvious, but really it's not, because you probably pinned that first version of the pin several months or even a year or so ago.

So, generally, people are just not going to notice. I've never had anyone tell me that they could tell that I've pinned the same pin three months later. Don't worry about that. You will have two of the same pin on your board and then after a certain amount of days, BoardBooster goes through, finds the pin that has the lower amount of re-pins, usually the older one and it will delete it, so you don't have duplicate pins. This keeps your board active without you needing to constantly find pins to schedule, and that's why it saves me so much time because I don't have to go through and find 100 pins per day to schedule like you would have to do with other scheduling programs or if you're just doing it by yourself with no program, it's going to take forever. With looping, you don't have to do that, you just keep your boards active by using content you've already pinned. Genius!

Best time to pin...

Now BoardBooster also has this cool thing, it's free, included in your plan called "Best Time to Pin". It basically just shows you a map of the different pinning times that you've shared pins at and it tells you which ones have the most re-pins. You can see on the left, I never pinned during that timeframe, maybe I should try it just to see, but my audience is usually online between about 8 AM to 11 PM. You can tell that there is a slight increase once we get more into the evening hours, that's when my audience is online more.

I make sure that I do some organic pinning around that time as well. I schedule, I loop but then I also do pin some things myself, I just go on Pinterest and pin a few things in the evening because that's when my audience is online. I don't want you to take this graphic to mean that everybody's audience is online in the evening, it really depends on who your people are. So if you sign up with BoardBooster then you're going to get this too. It's going to calculate based on your pins when your audience is online most, so that could be really helpful as well.

Now here's just a little glimpse of the pin doctor. After I have used pin doctor, it scans all of my boards and it found pins without links, with broken links, that links to suspicious websites etc. Then it just creates a list of all the pins that fall under those bad categories so that it's really easy for me to go through and delete or revise those pins. This is pretty awesome.

Now other Pinterest schedulers, I'm sure you've heard of other ones beside BoardBooster like Ahalogy, Buffer and ViralTag. They can all schedule pins, but the thing that I don't like about them is that none of these loop pins as far as I know, which is my absolute favorite feature and why I recommend using BoardBooster for looping. I'm very excited that Tailwind is committed to improving their features. I was prompted with a survey recently that eluded to them adding the looping feature which is incredibly exciting. They're not committing to a specific release date, though, so for now, BoardBooster is the only one that loops.

Now BoardBooster is not paying me, and I'm not affiliated with them. I just have had a lot of success with them and I wanted to share it with you guys. You can absolutely sign up with these other programs too but just know that you can't loop pins as far as I know, and looping pins is a thing that really saves me the most times because I can pin 100 pins per day and not have to find 100 things per day. If you are scheduling pins, you're going to have to find a lot of stuff every day and that's going to take a lot of time. So that's why don't use the other ones but I do know some people who like them so you could check them out, but I would start with BoardBooster especially because you are getting a free month.

Just to recap...

- Clean up your pins and boards. Basically you just want to get your Pinterest profile already for the impact of that BoardBooster is going to have on it. You want to clean it up, make it awesome.
- Sign up for the 100 days that you get for free with BoardBooster just for being an awesome Pinfinite Group student.
- Watch the training videos on BoardBooster to learn how to schedule and loop your BoardBooster pins. This is going to be a huge game changer for you, but make sure you watch the training videos so that you

are well acquainted with the piece of software before diving into it.
- Lastly, set up your BoardBooster account, publishing 100 pins per day.

CHAPTER TWELVE

Creating Organic Pins

You learned how to use the scheduler to schedule pins to your group boards, and now in this chapter, I'm going to show you how to schedule organic pins. By organic pins, I mean the content that you are pinning onto your boards, your regular boards, not the group boards but the ones that you created for your profile.

So Tailwind and BoardBooster have the capability to allow you to schedule pins to your boards so that they go out over the span of a few days or weeks which means that you can basically batch your pinning so that you just do it in one sitting and then you have content for weeks or months depending on how much you've actually scheduled.

You start on BoardBooster's homepage and then just click the scheduler at the top. Now if you haven't added any boards, this page might look blank. Scheduling in both apps is really easy. Just add boards to whichever scheduler you are in, editing your settings, and voila your pins that you've added to the queue are scheduled and ready to go.

In the settings, you may want to make some modifications or at least check what is set as default. For frequency, I recommend multiple pins per day being pinned onto your boards. For time settings, I recommend setting it to do basic pins per day, but this is really up to you. For boards that are very relevant and very consistent and popular for my brand, sometimes I up this to like seven, eight, nine pins per day. Because the 'color' board is a little less popular of the board, I don't use it all that often, I'm going to lower this to about three. It's really up to you.

If it is a board, let's say any of these boards in your very top row, you want those to be pinned to constantly. I would do at least five or six pins being scheduled to them per day, and it's okay if you don't meet that quota. So five or six per day, I'm just going to do three for the color board because this is, again, a board that I don't pin to super frequently. We're going to do three pins per day. Now spread between, you can pick the time settings here. I'm just going to do 9 AM to 10 PM; that's generally when my audience is online. I know it is a big time frame. You can adjust it based on when your audience is online. And again, BoardBooster has a cool feature under reports under the navigation bar. They have reports and you can see the best time to pin based on your audience. That's a good way to decide when your pins are going to be sent out.

Now pin on which dates, I usually do every day. Now here's the fun part, here's the important part. So because this is a regular board, your regular board on your account, not a group board, now we have source board. And what BoardBooster does is every time you add a board to the scheduler, it creates a feeder board, a secret feeder board on your account for all of your schedule boards.

Now it is up to you if you remove pins from the source board or you keep it on the source board, the source board being the secret feeder board. If you do decide to keep it on the source board, you can choose – so after all the pins are published, so all, let's say 20 pins that I pin to my secret feeder board, you can either stop or you can start over. It will re-pin all those pins to your secret feeder board. It's not generally a good thing to have duplicate pins on the same board, so I wouldn't recommend starting over on your own personal boards, I would just remove it from the source board because you don't really need to use it again. And then you can click save and you are set.

So now all you need to do is when you are on Pinterest,

instead of pinning to like this board you are going to pin to your feeder board and that is going to pin things out. BoardBooster is going to pin it out for you over the span of several days based on how many pins per day you have scheduled.

That's how you schedule pins using BoardBooster to your own brand boards, super easy. And then all you have to do is spend about 30 to 40 minutes per week pinning to these feeder boards and then it will go out, all those pins will go out during the week and you don't have to worry about Pinterest again.

CHAPTER THIRTEEN

Looping Pins with BoardBooster

In this chapter, I'm going to be showing you how to use BoardBooster to loop your pins which is a feature you are about to fall madly in love with. Now this is the feature that I love about BoardBooster. It is what sets it apart from other Pinterest schedulers out there because it's not a scheduler. Looping your pins is not scheduling them, it's a whole different ballgame.

Let me show you what it is and why it rocks my freaking world. You just want to loop boards that are super relevant to your audience and to your brand. You don't want to loop any boards that are a little iffy or aren't that important to your brand because looping is where a majority of the pins that you share are going to come from. You want to make sure that you are only sharing pins that are super relevant to your brand especially because you are going to be sharing them so much through looping.

Pick multiple pins per day, which just means that multiple pins are going to be looped on this board per day. I don't really see a reason why you would want to do one or less pins per day, but maybe you have a reason. Time settings, I honestly just do basic. It's really up to you if you do advanced. Advanced, you can do a couple pinning windows, you can change the schedule on weekends. This is really just if your audience is online at different times. So pay attention to when your audience is online, if they are then you can set up your time settings to really match when they are online, but I do basic because my audience is generally online between about 8 AM to 10 PM.

Regarding the number of pins per day - the number of pins that you loop per day is dependent on two things in my opinion. Number one, it is dependent on how relevant that board is to your brand. If it's one of the most relevant boards where this board is particularly important to your brand and to your audience, then I would up this number to like seven, eight, nine. If it's a little bit less relevant, then maybe like five or four. Then number two, you want this number to be higher if you have a lot of pins on that board. So if you have like 500, 600, 1000 pins on the board, then it's okay to have a higher number here. If you only have 50 pins on this board, then you're going to want to do a much smaller number like two or three. So here is why.

When you loop pins, you are taking your oldest pins from this particular board and you are re-pinning them to the same board. You are going to have two of the same pin on the same board. And what this does is basically pull out your old content, re-pin it so that you have fresh content constantly being pinned onto your account, and then you have the option to delete the pin that performed the worst basically. Let me explain that in just a second, but basically, you are pulling your old content from the board and BoardBooster is automatically re-pinning it for you. You don't even have to do anything and you are constantly having new content – not really new because you pinned it way back in the day, but new content being pinned onto your boards through looping. So you are just looping your old content that you have already pinned.

Again, for pins per day, if it is super relevant to your brand and you have a lot of pins on that board, then you want this number to be higher like six, seven or eight, maybe even nine or ten if you have a lot of pins and it is very relevant to your brand. If it's a smaller board like this one, only has about 40 or 50 pins, I'm just going to do let's say three pins per day.

And then spread between, we're going to do 8 AM to 10 PM, pin every day. Pin selection method; oldest to newest. I think that is important because otherwise you are going to be re-pinning your newest content right after you pinned it. That doesn't really make sense, so do oldest to newest.

Then here's the fun part. So with automatic de-duplication, I would highly encourage you to enable this. What this does is after you get to pick a period o f time down here, I usually do one week, so after seven days, it's going to compare those two pins. The old pin that you pinned way back in the day and then the new version of it that BoardBooster re-pinned for you, it is going to compare those two and then it is going to delete the one that has the least amount of re-pins so that you don't have duplicate content on your account, but so that you are constantly looping your pins so you still have fresh content always being published.

Another cool feature is protection for viral duplicates. I usually enable this, and what this does is that if let's say both of your pins go viral and they both get 50 pins or more in the span of seven days, then we will just keep them both because those are really good numbers and we don't want to lose either one of those pins even if one of them has less. It will keep both of them if you enable viral duplicates which I do, I usually put 50 as this number. And then protection for pins with comments, I disable that because I can just read the comments before the pin is deleted and respond to the person before it disappears.

What is super great about all these features is I'm pinning about 100 pins but I don't even have to do anything because it is just pinning content that I've already shared in the past. And you might be wondering like is this annoying to my followers who are following me and seeing the same content over and over again? But I've got to tell you that it's not and I've never had a complaint, and the reason is because I've so many pins on these boards already, that people just don't notice when they see a pin the second or third time around because it takes about like a month or even more than that to actually get through all of these pins.

That's why you want to set the pin number to a good number that makes sense with how many pins are on that board. I have a lot of pins on my blogging tips board which is why I have the most pins going out to this board per day, and this is also very, very relevant to my brand, so that's why I also have so many pins going out to my blogging tips board every day. Now it really depends on which boards are most relevant to your brand and how many pins you have on those boards already to decide how many pins you are going to share per day on that board.

Looping is just a really awesome feature of BoardBooster because it's going to grow your account. Remember the smart feed is looking for pinners who share quality content constantly on their account. So if you are looping 98 pins per day, then my friend, you're going to grow your account like crazy and attract the right people because if you are selecting very relevant to your brand boards to loop – so again, all of these are very relevant to my brand and my ideal audience, then you're going to be sharing a lot of content that attracts the right people to your account. Just by doing this, just by looping boards every day where I don't have to do anything, my account is growing by hundreds every single month and my traffic is growing too, because on all of these boards as well, I have a mix of other people's content and my own content. So it's looping pins that are not just other people's pins, but also things that are from my website.

I've always got some of my own pins interspersed in here and there so that we are always driving traffic back to my site and then because I'm pinning so much, it's growing my Pinterest account which like exponentially grows everything, brings more people to my account and to my blog and website. Looping is an awesome feature, I love it and it is going to grow your account and your website like crazy.

CHAPTER FOURTEEN

Pinterest Analytics

In this section, we're getting a little bit techy because we are analyzing your Pinterest Analytics.

Now just upfront a note, you must sign up for a free business account to access Pinterest Analytics. If you don't have a business account, you might be looking at this section and this section and kind of be wondering what the heck is going on. So make sure that you sign up for a business account. This is explained in an earlier section, but you should do it before proceeding, otherwise this is going to be gibberish to you. It's really easy to set up your account though. So just go back to the previous section where we talk about setting up your business account and you should be all good to go.

Before we get into this section, I need to tell you that talking about analytics is not the most exciting thing in the world. It's a little bit dry, not too fun, like some of the other chapters you've read, but it's essential to learn.

Alright, so to view your analytics you go to your profile page and then click the little gear symbol on the top right and scroll down until you see analytics and click that. Remember you need a business account in order to access that. Now this is the landing page you're going to see, the Pinterest Analytics landing page. If you click more, next to any of those three boxes, it's going to take you to three different pages. It's important to have your Pinterest analytics pulled up on your computer while you read this so you fully understand.

First, we're going to be talking about your Pinterest profile, so let's click the more button next to your Pinterest profile and we can view the stats about your profile. Now just real quick, you can see that there are some different stats right here on the front page. I honestly don't keep too much of a track of these different stats. It's nice to know occasionally how many people are viewing your profile, how many people are viewing your pins, but you kind of want to see if these are increasing or decreasing by a lot, but I don't pay a lot of attention to these. I usually think it is best to just click through and look at the actual stats, the more specific stats than paying super close attention

LEARN PINTEREST STRATEGY

to these vague numbers.

Let's get to it, your Pinterest profile. Now these are the boards and pins that your followers enjoy the most. We want a healthy balance of clicks and re-pins which means that they are power pins. This is going to make a whole lot more sense once I show you the screen that your Pinterest profile analytics will take you to, but if they are not clicking then it's not creating viral sharing, and if they are only re-pinning, then no one is actually reading your content.

Now if we go to your Pinterest profile, that first little box, then we have top pin impressions. You can see there is a little navigation bar at the top, says impressions, re-pins, clicks and all time. If we click impressions, then we have some different columns there which also says impressions, clicks, re-pins, likes. I just like to take a look at this screen and it shows you your top pin impressions from the last 30 days. Now take note all of my top pin impressions are rich pins, and yours should be, as well. Don't worry, you'll get there.

You can see that on the farthest right corner where it says pin type, that box with an "R" in it, that means that they are rich pins. If you didn't believe me that rich pins are important, then girl or boy, because there's some boys in this course too, rich pins are very important. They show that you have a high-quality pin. I just want to point that out. And also, in case you're wondering what the "P" is, that means it's a pin that is promoted.

Now here's the big thing that I want you to pay attention to, that I was talking about in the previous slide. Compare your clicks versus your re-pins to craft better descriptions.

If I wanted to boost my re-pin rate, I could do a few different things. I could promote the pin to promote it to aim to get more re-pins. I could craft a better description that encourages people to re-pin, remember adding that call to action. So there are a couple of different things that you could do.

Now if the pin was getting- let's see if any of them-no, it looks like all of these have more clicks than re-pins, but if any of them were getting say more re-pins and not so many click throughs, then that definitely means that I could create a better description to get people to click through the pin to actually visit my website. So again, creating a call to action like "click through to read the full article" or even creating a new pin image, just like my old one but adding a call to action button like we talked about in the pinnable pins section, where you're adding like little graphic on to your image saying click through or click to read or something like that where you're encouraging people to actually click through and read your article. Because it's nice to have re-pins but it's not so nice if people actually aren't clicking through to read your article. Those are just a few different things you can do by analyzing this data, the top pin impressions.

Now we also have top board impressions if you scroll down. So these are the topics your audience loves. Now these are all of your boards, remember this is your Pinterest profile.

LEARN PINTEREST STRATEGY

Take a look at your top boards, are they on brand, are they relevant to what you're trying to create, that focus that you are trying to create on your website. If I look at mine, they're pretty darn relevant because I'm aiming at bloggers and entrepreneurs. So we have 'blogging tips', 'entrepreneur tips', 'dream office', 'blogging tips and tricks resources'. There are a couple in there that are a little bit random like home decor or words which is like quotes, but most of them are pretty on-brand and relevant to my audience.

So I'm making sure that my top boards are ones that are going to attract my ideal audience. And again, create a call to action specific to your needs, re-pins versus clicks. So depending on which boards have a lot of clicks versus re-pins, remember you want a healthy balance of both, trying to create those descriptions on the pins within that board, that are going to kind of up the clicks if you're low on clicks or up the re-pins if you're low on re-pins.

For example, my 'dream office' board, the very bottom almost, dream office board has hardly any clicks but it has quite a lot of re-pins. So I could create different kinds of descriptions to really add that call to action and get people to click through and read more of those posts because it's really not doing any good to pin things that board because people aren't clicking through to the actual post and reading them.

Now if you click all time at the top, you can see which pins rank the highest in search, so best in search, pins that rank higher in search. What do these pins have in common? Now these aren't necessarily my pins, pretty much none of these pins are from my actual website, they are just pins that I pinned, but take a look at the pins that show up in this best in search section, because these pins are the ones that are power pins according to Pinterest, ones that are doing really well in search, that something about these pins someone is doing right.

Now moving on to the second section, your audience. Your audience section only has two subsections; demographics and interests. If we click the very first one that says demographics, it shows us basically where our followers and our pinners, our audience is coming from; so which countries, which cities, what languages and what gender. So as you can see, most of my audience comes from the US and specifically Los Angeles or big cities in general, and also most of my audience is female.

These kinds of demographics can be really helpful especially if you have like a product based business where you are shipping things out, maybe you see that a lot of people are re-pinning your stuff from the UK, but you don't ship to the UK. So maybe you want to change that because currently, you have a big market for the UK but if you're not shipping to them then you could be losing out on a lot of business. Taking a look at your demographics and just seeing if there is any way that you could incorporate these demographics into your blog or business.

Now if you click the interests section next to demographics, it's going to take you to a screen. This shows your interests, what your audience is into. These are the topics that your peeps are searching for the most. So for most of them, what I write about blogging, social media, entrepreneur, that's kind of all clumped together under technology. There isn't really a great topic to pick for that one but I have to pick technology, there is like a robot or something there which is why technology is so high on mine, but this represents the whole view of your target market, beyond just what you are selling.

I might write about blogging, social media tips, but my audience is also really interested in home decor, recipes, home improvement, inspirational quotes etc. So it kind of just gives me a more in-depth picture of who my audience is so that I can create like a brand story around my brand which really appeals to my audience. Now I don't recommend taking these interests and then pinning about all of them or blogging about all of them, that's just going to ruin your blog's focus or your business' focus, but rather I just want you to take a look at these interests and see how they all come together to create this unique type of person.

Now under the interests section as well, we have this really cool part where it says boards: pinner boards with lots of your pins. These are basically boards that other people have created that tend to have a lot of your own pins on them. I think this is an awesome little analytics section that Pinterest provides you because it shows the top people who really dig what you are doing.

These could be people that you could reach out to, to collaborate with or maybe they are your ideal customer. So if you are selling something and they are constantly pinning your products, then maybe you could get like an ideal customer profile from them, really analyze who this person is, how you can add their interests to what you are selling or what you are creating. So study these people.

What can they teach you? Who are they? What's their job? Where do they live? What do they do? Why do they care so much about what you are putting out there? You can also find most likely on brand content to pin from these boards. If you are running out of things to pin or you are looking for awesome content in a pinch, then you can probably go to these boards under your audience interests boards and find a lot of cool stuff to pin that's totally on brand because most of these boards, it looks like talk about blogging business tips which is so central to my brand. So it would be really easy for me to just peek through all these boards and schedule a bunch of stuff onto my Pinterest.

Now lastly, we have audience interests: brands. These are the businesses your audience engages. Generally, these are your big name competitors, so what do they say about your audience. These are kind of like who you would be in 10 years, not 10 years, one year, two years – 10 years is crazy talk. These are your big name competitors. So what do they say about your audience? What can you glean from studying these competitors?

Now we're going to check out the last section, activity from your website. We have impressions, re-pins, clicks, original pins, all time – we have all this stuff. Try clicking on "impressions". We have top pin impressions and boards with top pin impressions. Now remember, these are just the pins from your website, not just things that you pin, but specifically things from your website. It shows you the top pins from your site with the most impressions, re-pins and clicks.

Now you can use this to analyze which types of content drive the most traffic. This is an awesome way to study your content, what you are putting on Pinterest, to see if people like what you write about often or maybe you'll see a post in there that you didn't even know people really liked or that really got a lot of traction on Pinterest, but all of a sudden, it's one of your top pin impression pins of the last 30 days and you are like, "oh wow maybe I should write more content like that, because clearly people are liking it". It could surprise you to see what you find on these, the top pin impressions or boards with top impressions.

Boards with top impressions similarly will show you what your audience, the specific topics that they really enjoy learning about. So definitely take a look at this, the activity from your website and then impressions to see what people are really falling in love with the most.

Now most re-pins, if we take a look at the column where it

says re-pins, most re-pins generally mean that that type of content or that post inspires users. They don't necessarily need to click through to read it, but they want to save it for later because they aspire to be like whatever that post is selling. Now most clicks is indicative of users that want to learn more and/or are ready to buy.

So maybe they really want to learn about that topic or you are talking about a product and they are like I need that, so they click through to either read your article or buy your product. It is important to kind of take into account clicks versus re-pins because you want to see, are people just aspiring to be like this, they will save it for later, for one day or are they actually clicking through to take action today because we really want them to take action, we do want re-pins, but we don't just want re-pins. Take a look at your post, see which ones are getting clicks, see which ones are getting re-pins and see which ones are just getting the most impressions overall.

Some examples...

If you have a product pin with lots of re-pins, but not as many clicks, so it's getting re-pinned a lot, but people aren't clicking through to read it, then here are a couple of things you need to do. You need to work on your pin's description, so add keywords to target the people who would want to click through. So maybe your description is lacking, maybe the people who your product pin is geared towards can't find your pin because it doesn't have the proper keywords in the description. Add those key words so that the right people are finding it. And then add a call to action to your pin image and your pin description. You're going to have to create a new image and then re-pin it if you want to do that route, but creating a call to action to your image and your pin description, like "click through to check out this product" or "click through to read the full article".

Now if you have a valuable blog post with lots of clicks but few re-pins, so every time somebody sees this blog post, they click through to read it, but most people are not re-pinning it, so not as many people are seeing it as could see it. If that's happening, lots of clicks but few re-pins, then add a call to action in the description encouraging people to re-pin it, like just tell them re-pin this post if you found it useful or re-pin this post and then click through to read or you could also promote your pin to get more re-pins, so promoted things as an option again, where you can promote it specifically to get more re-pins.

That could be a great option if you're getting a lot of clicks but few re-pins because it shows that you have a post that people really like, they probably click through to read it and then forget to re-pin it. So you just got to give them that call to action or try promoted posts to actually get them to see it more often.

Now lastly, we have best in search from your site. If we click all time and then we will scroll down and see best in search, these are the pins that rank higher in search. These are again power pins. Now which of your pins are ranking the highest? So again, thinking about the smart feed. These are the pins that always pop up at the top when somebody is scrolling through their smart feed. So why?

As you can see these all seem to have a description, so take a look, see what keywords you are adding and make sure that if you want a pin to pop up as best in search, you are adding those descriptions to your pins. So overall, your analytics will show you what your audience enjoys the most and the types of content you should create more of because clearly they love it, if there are any gaps in your content, so things that your audience is interested in but you are not providing. So things that they could like, maybe they fall under a certain topic but you just aren't really writing about them. And which pins could do better if you adjust the descriptions or pin images. Remember that call to action, re-pins versus clicks.

Just to recap...

- Sign up for a business account; you need your business account in order to access analytics.
- Explore your Pinterest analytics, so there are just tons of different things that you can take a look at. We covered most of them in this section, but really explore your analytics to see all the different stats that you have access to.
- Look for the content your audience enjoys most and then create more of it, super easy right?

- And then also look for the content that can be improved to better reach your goals. So basically just making sure that you are creating content that is hyper relevant and hyper useful to your ideal audience, so using your analytics to figure out what type of content that is.

CHAPTER FIFTEEN

Using Google Analytics

So whether you can consider yourself a data nerd or not, I have a feeling you're going to enjoy this section. We're talking about analyzing Pinterest using Google Analytics. Let's get started.

What is Google Analytics?...

Google Analytics is a free analytics software which can tell you some pretty darn in-depth stats about your site. It can be really useful for seeing which pins are getting the most views and converting the most visitors into subscribers or buyers. If you don't have Google Analytics set up on your site already, I highly, highly suggest that you get on that.

How to install it...

I'll just briefly go through how you can get Google Analytics on your site. It's really easy to do. It is very easy as you can tell. Visit google.com/analytics, to create an account for your site.

Now when you create an account, you need to insert a tracking code on to your website from your Google Analytics account. That's how they kind of talk to each other. On WordPress, install the Google Analytics plug-in on your WordPress site. Then in Google Analytics, go to the admin > tracking info > tracking code and copy your tracking ID into the Google Analytics plug-in and you are done. It's super easy. If you are more familiar with the back end of a website, then you can do it without using this plug-in, but this is more of the simple way to add it to your website in case you are unfamiliar with more of the kind of back end of a website.

So this is the super easy way to add Google Analytics and then you can go to your Google Analytics account and pretty soon you'll start to see the stats rolling in. You can see how many visitors you are getting, which pages have the highest amount of page views. Those are really basic statistics, but Google Analytics can tell you a whole bunch of really interesting things about your site. So definitely get it.

Which posts get the most love?...

This is one of my favorite ways to check out how Pinterest is doing on your site or with your site. To see which posts receive the most traffic from Pinterest, go to acquisition, social, overview and then Pinterest, so acquisition, social, overview, Pinterest – and from there, you can see which posts on your website or which pages on your website are getting the most traffic from Pinterest. This can be really useful for a lot of reasons. How to use this info? Why is it useful?

Now that you know which posts receive the most traffic from Pinterest, you can see what your audience enjoys the most and create more just like it. If you notice a trend that certain posts are getting more views than other posts from Pinterest, then you can make an effort to share more of those posts on your Pinterest account or even just pin the same images more than once; pinning them every week or every couple weeks because obviously your Pinterest followers like those types of posts.

Now if you sell products, this is also a great way to see which products you should create more of so that you can promote them on Pinterest. You can also add content upgrades and better paths in these posts to ensure that these visitors are going to stick around. You could also add more info about your products or affiliate links to generate more of an income. Basically, once you know which posts are bringing the most traffic, then you just want to pimp out those posts. You need to add content upgrades, so adding a way for somebody to subscribe to your email list once they reach that post, and better paths, so what I mean by that is having more of a goal in mind with your post.

You could add affiliate links where you are getting people to come to that post and then they are purchasing something, so you make a commission or you are adding more info about your products or you are weaving in more back links to previous posts on your site to keep people clicking around more. So really think about what kind of paths you can add to your post. We talked about paths in a previous unit, but they are a really great way to think about what you want your visitors to do once they reach your post.

Now if this is an older post, which it might be because Pinterest is a search engine and SEO (Search Engine Optimization) usually takes a few months to really start booming. If this is an older post, then it makes sense because Pinterest sometimes takes a little while to really bring you a lot of traffic on those older posts. If it's an older post, update it to make sure it is evergreen and on brand.

You want to make sure that this is timeless content and that your images are on brand. I can't tell you how many posts I had to go back through and update because my images were just not looking good. They were from way back in the day when I had no idea what I was doing, but they are getting a lot of traffic because again, SEO takes a while to start booming. My older posts were starting to bring in more and more traffic because they've been around for a long time, but the images were just not very good. I updated those images, re-pinned those posts onto Pinterest so that I could now get traffic to that old image and to the new image that I pinned, so that post was doing even better than before.

Which pins work the hardest?...

To see which pins drive the most traffic to your site – so before we were talking about which pages got the most traffic, now we are talking about which pins, specifically which pin images drive the most traffic to your site. To find that out, you go to acquisition, all traffic, referrals and then pinterest.com. It's going to take you to a page that looks like this, so we have the little referral path and you need to copy that path into your browser after pinterest.com. You can see that it's just the ending of the URL. You need to copy your referral path ending after pinterest.com and then you will be able to see which pin that is, the actual pin image will pop up. You can see which pin that is, to see which pin is driving the most traffic to your site.

How to use this information...

Each of these referral paths is a pin that your visitors clicked in order to get your site. By visiting the links in the referral paths, you can see which pins are driving the most traffic to you. Now analyze these pins; do they have anything in common, are you targeting specific keywords in their descriptions, what do the images look like? See if there are any patterns. Maybe you are surprised to find that a certain type of image is constantly bringing the most traffic or maybe they are all images with people in them or maybe it is a certain type of text that you tried out on your images or maybe it's just a certain topic. More likely, it's probably just a certain type of topic. So figure out which ones are bringing the most traffic to your site and if you can find any patterns in that data. Now knowing which pins work the hardest is a great way to make sure you create more pins and posts just like them.

Just to recap...

- Sign up for a Google Analytics account. You can easily sign up for an account within a matter of minutes.
- Add to the Google Analytics code to your site. There's a WordPress plugin that you can install as well to make it super easy.
- View which posts get the most love from Pinterest and that's going to tell you which types of posts you should create more of, which types of products your audience is really liking.
- View which pins drive the most traffic to your site so that you can create more pin images just like them and also pin topics on the same topic.

- And then use this data to enhance your content and Pinterest strategy, so pretty much just everything that we've gone through. Use that data to enhance your content and your strategies so that you can really bring in more of the right visitors.

CHAPTER SIXTEEN

Developing Your Email List

First of all why your email list is important? Because Pinterest is a fantastic way to help you grow your email list so I can't leave this out of the section. I got to tell you how you do it successfully.

Why your email list is so important...

- Number one, it's direct. You can get in touch with your followers when you want to. You're not reliant on your audience checking their social media accounts or visiting your blog. You basically can get inside of their email inbox whenever you want. So if you have a new blog post up or you are running a sale or you have a new product that you are launching, this is a fantastic way to be able to get into their inbox so that they are seeing this new thing that you want to tell them about and they are not missing out on it, because if you just post it on your blog or your social media, there's a big chance that they are not going to see it. Getting in their inbox is a sure-fire way to make sure that they see your updates.

- Number two, you own your email list. Technically you don't own your following on social media and actually, you don't even own your following on Pinterest, but you do own your email list and it can't be taken away from you. People sign up to your email list and you have those people's names and emails that you can keep forever. You can continue to email those people even if Pinterest, Facebook, Twitter and Instagram all decide to close up shop. This is a really big deal because you want to make sure that if you're putting all of this effort into growing your blog or online business, that you have a tangible asset to be able to contact your followers and customers.

Now let me take you back to the big Facebook crisis that happened a few years ago. A few years ago, Facebook changed its algorithm for pages. Prior to changing its algorithm, you could post something on your Facebook page and it would just go bananas. People were getting a lot of traffic from Facebook, they were making sales. And then Facebook changed their algorithm, showing you that you do not own Facebook and now you're going to have to pay for Facebook ads if you want your content to be seen. So all those people who spent their time growing their Facebook page following were now left in the dust. I don't want that to happen to you which is why I think your email list should be the number one thing that you focus on growing.

So bottom line, no one can take your email list away from you. It's not dependent on algorithms or some other company's decisions. You should always be growing an email list in order to reach your audience and maintain your brand. Email lists are also more personal. A person's inbox is kind of like their virtual home. It means something when they invite you into it. It's almost like giving you their phone number, so they want to stay in contact with you and that is a big deal. When someone likes you on Instagram or likes your page on Facebook, I don't think it means quite as much as somebody willing to give you their sacred email address. It also allows you to connect in a deeper way. So within your emails that you send to your list, you can connect to your audience in a more personal way. You can share vulnerable stories. You can really get real with your audience. This allows the deeper connection and especially because you're reading them inside of their virtual home which just builds that connection even more, but it is overall more personal.

A fun fact: email lists have higher conversion rates than other types of things out there. If you are selling something or ever plan to, an email list is essential because it converts those people, potential customers into actual paying customers. Basically, bottom line, if you post the same offering on your Instagram, in a blog post and in an email, you will almost always get the highest percentage of buyers from your email. This should be a game changer alert for you if you are selling anything online.

Just to recap...

- Your email list is essential especially if you do or plan to sell something online.
- Develop your own email list and use it.
- It has higher conversion rates than social media and blog posts and it's proven to be an excellent place to connect with your audience.

CHAPTER SEVENTEEN

Content Upgrades

Now if you want to grow your list, this section is going to be huge for you because we're talking about how to use content upgrades to grow your list with Pinterest.

What is a content upgrade?...

Maybe you haven't heard this term before. A content upgrade is a download that you offer people in exchange for their email address. It upgrades a piece of content that you created by adding additional information for free. If that doesn't make sense, don't worry, I've got some examples for you.

Content upgrades can come in almost any form that you can think of; things like checklist, tutorials, workbooks, mini e-books, free email courses etc. Basically if you can think of a way to up level your content or add some extra value for your readers or visitors, then you can turn it into a content upgrade. Some examples are a free email course-now you can see I actually put a content upgrade on my Pinterest image to show people that if they click through, they're going to get access to this awesome freebie. Here we got my free email course. Here I created content upgrades that are spreadsheets. Here I created a free media kit and here is a free workbook, or a free cheat sheet. You can see that there are a number of different things that you can add for free as a content upgrade.

- You want to focus on providing extra value. Create something useful that helps people take action and gives them a way to dive deeper into your content because maybe they read your blog post or listened to your podcast or watched your YouTube video and they loved it, but now they want to know how do I actually put this into action or how do I take this to the next level. Your content upgrade is a way for you to add that extra value by letting people know that you've got a worksheet or a video or some other piece of content that's going to add extra value for them. It can also give even more content or tips.
- A pro tip: your content upgrade should always have a

takeaway or end goal. What do you want someone to get out of this content upgrade that you're creating? What's the point of them signing up for it? So if you can answer that question, then you can be sure that you've created a really useful content upgrade.

How do content upgrades and Pinterest go together?...

Here is the formula. Pinterest and everything you just learned in this book will drive a ton of traffic to your website. That's just the way it works. Then if you add content upgrades to your content, your podcasts, your blog posts, your videos, then that new traffic you're getting from Pinterest will then subscribe to your email list. It is amazingly effective and it runs on autopilot.

When I started doing this, I started implementing my Pinterest system, I started adding content upgrades to a lot of my blog posts, I grew my email list by about 8000 subscribers within one month. Within three months, I had grown my list more than 45,000 subscribers, and in 4 months of combining my Pinterest system with adding content upgrades, I grew my list to 50,000 subscribers. That's crazy, 3-4 months, 50,000 subscribers and it's largely due to this system that I just taught you.

How often should you create content upgrades?...

Well adding them to every piece of content is ideal. That's what you want to shoot for, but obviously that's a pretty lofty goal and content upgrades can take a bit of time to create. Instead you can also reuse content upgrades on different blog posts or create something more general that you use all over the place. It's not just on one blog post or it's not just created for that particular blog post, but maybe you create a free email course or you create something that you can use on multiple blog posts and also in other places on your website. This is a great way to reuse your content upgrades but still get those people signing up to your email list from Pinterest.

Where to start...

Where should you start if you have a lot of content, if you have no content? It doesn't matter. Where should you start with creating content upgrades? I recommend going straight to your most popular posts. This way you can capitalize on the posts that are already getting momentum and have a larger audience to convert because if you know that people are interested in these popular posts, then you know that they are probably interested in that topic. If you add on some sort of upgrade, worksheet, free email course, a cheat sheet, a checklist- whatever it is, then you can be pretty sure that people are going to be interested in it since they were already interested in the topic of that blog post.

After creating content upgrades for your 5 to 10 most popular posts, then you can begin creating content upgrades for new posts, but you want to start with those most popular posts because they are already getting traffic. Now to find your most popular posts, just go into Google Analytics and then search by behavior, site content, all pages. You can see it down there at the bottom. That's going to give you a list of your most popular posts on your website.

How do you create a content upgrade?...

You could use a variety of design programs like Apple Pages or Microsoft Word, or you could do it in Adobe InDesign. It doesn't really matter which program you use, anything that allows you to save your content upgrade as a PDF if you're going to be sending some sort of worksheet. Otherwise, you could use your email service provider to send out something like a free email course or free video course, totally up to you.

How do you send this coveted content upgrade?...

Well, you want to set up your email service provider so that your content upgrade is sent in the email that they receive after registering to your email list. This is super easy to do in MailChimp, and MailChimp is my recommendation to most people who are starting an email list or even people who are in this kind of intermediate level of using their email list because it has just the right amount of functionality for most people but it's still very easy to use.

Just to recap...

- Content upgrades are a very powerful way to grow your list with Pinterest.
- You create something that adds value to your content in order to gain subscribers.

Again, I use this same system to grow my list to 50,000 people in 4 months. So it can be done and it can be done fast.

Conclusion

I really hope that you have enjoyed learning more about Pinterest and developing a strategy around it to grow your blog and business. Pinterest is such a powerful tool and I know that if you implement what you learned in this book, you will be immensely successful as a blogger, writer, marketer, and entrepreneur.

Thank you for reading the book and be sure to share it with others that are not avid pinners (yet)!

~ Kerrie Legend ~

About the Author

Kerrie Legend has an undying love for the deep sea, sailing, raising goats, farming and raising her family of six boys alongside her husband of over 10 years. She is an avid writer and blogger at kerrielegend.com, a site for bloggers and writers to learn and understand social media strategy. She is a course presenter and online educator. As a graphic designer, Kerrie works full-time from home for entrepreneurs designing graphics, while homeschooling her boys. She is a proud supporter of homeschooling education, spends her days teaching bright minds and engaging in playful dinosaur adventures with Legos and Thomas the Train.

She and her husband also blog at Mancave Mayhem, a site for interior design and shopping ideas for building the ultimate shecave or mancave. Her husband works fulltime from home as a farmer and carpenter, designing furniture and home solutions from repurposed wood resources.

Acknowledgments

Thank you to my family for bearing with me in my late-night stints in writing, for understanding when "mommy has a deadline" and "mommy needs to write". Thanks to my husband for helping me make it all work so I can pursue my passion in designing and writing.

Thanks for reading! Please add a short review on Amazon and let me know what you thought!

As an online reviewer, I am always looking for ways to support my peers in the writing community in positive ways. I'd appreciate hearing what you loved about the book but also what you'd like to see me expand on. When I review books, I always try to find something genuinely positive to say, and I'd appreciate the same from you, my reader, as well. Thank you for taking the time to read and learn. You are appreciated!

Made in the USA
Middletown, DE
14 February 2020